USING NONBROADCAST VIDEO IN THE CHURCH

USING NONBROADCAST VIDEO IN THE CHURCH

DANIEL W. HOLLAND
J. ASHTON NICKERSON
TERRY VAUGHN

Judson Press ® Valley Forge

Using Nonbroadcast Video in the Church

Library of Congress Cataloging in Publication Data

Holland, Daniel W.
  Using nonbroadcast video in the church.

  Includes bibliographical references.
  1. Television in religion.   I.   Nickerson, J.
Ashton, joint author.   II.   Vaughn, Terry, joint author.
III.   Title.
BV656.3.H64   253'.028   80-15004
ISBN 0-8170-0895-0

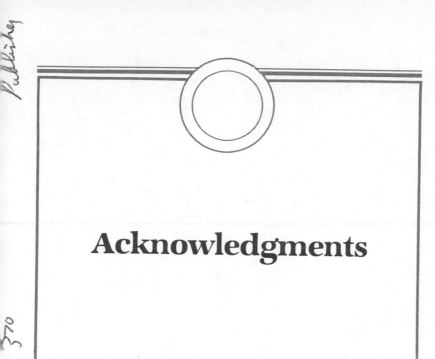

Acknowledgments

For one week during the summer of 1978 nearly 150 Christian communicators met in Toronto to learn from one another and sharpen the communications skills they use to spread Christ's gospel in the twentieth century. Twenty-five of those people were involved in a "track" called the Television Un-Broadcast Experience or TUBE. The twenty-page "study paper" that came out of that week's learnings forms the basis for this book. The authors gratefully acknowledge their contributions to this volume.

Participants at TUBE '78 were: Diane Armendt, George Cox, Jim Forsythe, Donald Hill, Carlos Mooney, Grayce Phillips, Kenneth Scott, Jr., Michael Loy Vandiver, Gwendolyn Arbuckle, Sr. Luke Crawford, Sr. Suzanne Hackmiller, Joseph Isenhower, Jr., Bruce Mosher, William Rathbun, Charles Sumners, Jr., Norm Wilson, Emily Deeter, Alan Harley, Thomas Lowry, Gary Richardson, Grayley Taylor.

Our thanks also to the Reverend David Pomeroy, Communications Commission, National Council of Churches, for his work which forms the basis of the bibliography in this volume.

Contents

1

Nonbroadcast Video and the Church

Just as the first-century church learned through Pentecost to communicate the gospel in new languages, the church of today must learn new languages to communicate with its world. One of those new languages is the emerging revolution of electronic communication.

A vast array of new technologies is greeting the inhabitants of "Spaceship Earth." Audio-cassette recorders and portable radios reach even the most remote areas of earth. Satellite technology will soon offer television and other communications media to the Eskimos in the Arctic and the hill tribes of Thailand. School children are given courses in "visual literacy," and many high schools have complete color TV studios. Elementary school students produce high quality Super-8 films and even videotapes.

Home computers offer the same services for a few hundred dollars that once took a room full of equipment and millions of dollars. America is well on its way to becoming a "wired nation," and predictions of computers in homes talking with computers in businesses, fire companies, banks, and police stations are now realities.

American society is increasingly dependent on electronic technology. This dependence will continue to grow as our society changes in other ways. Fuel shortages will make business travel more and more

9

expensive. Companies are already beginning to use closed-circuit TV to hold meetings at a great savings in time and money. Electronic "mail" is being used instead of the costly, personnel intensive, type-written inter- and intraoffice communications.

Banking is also increasingly dependent on the new technology. It is now possible in many American cities for an individual to bank entirely by phone. The touch-tone phone becomes, in effect, a mini-terminal for the central banking computer.

NEW TECHNOLOGY AND THE CHURCH

But where is the church in all of this? Sixteen-millimeter films have been around for one hundred years, radio for fifty, and TV for thirty-five; yet the church school curriculum, continuing education, leadership development, and mission interpretation remain, for the most part, mired in the ink of the Gutenberg Galaxy.

Like other social institutions the church often resists new tech-nologies and methodologies until the pressure becomes so great that it has no other choice but to change. This characteristic provides an excellent balance against fads and gives needed continuity, but it can also become an excuse for seldom acting innovatively when a new and useful technology for communicating the gospel arises.

When the church has embraced a new technology, it often has used it only to support its existing way of doing things. Radio, and then TV, were seen early in their development as evangelistic tools. Unfortunately, instead of developing new styles to fit the medium of electronic communication, the church often tries to fit the older form of song and sermon into the medium of sight, sound, and movement.

As American, and indeed world, society changes in the context of vast technological developments, the pressure for the church to develop new ways of communicating the gospel to that society grows. One of the new ways the church can communicate to this new society is through the medium of nonbroadcast video. Sometimes called "pri-vate video," nonbroadcast video (NBV) is usually defined as any use of video primarily designed for small groups and targeted for a specific audience. It is "narrowcasting" as opposed to "broadcasting." In more technical terms, nonbroadcast video refers to the use of the television medium without transmitting the video signal over the air. In this sense, NBV includes direct camera-to-monitor applications or camera-to-re-corder applications.

Broadcast video is a very expensive proposition, and for that reason the local church and most denominations are limited by economics to very little work in this area. Broadcasting, while it has its uses for the mission of the local church, will continue to be out of reach for most congregations. NBV, on the other hand, offers a versatility and economic incentive that will allow many local churches, regional organizations, and denominations to use it.

Of course, just because a new technology has been developed does not necessarily mean that it will be utilized by a majority of the society into which it is introduced. Economic and social frameworks must be taken into account. Many promising technologies have been abandoned because either the society into which they were introduced was not ready, or the economics of the technology prohibited further development until a more realistic technology was developed. Books were available only to a few wealthy persons until the invention of movable type when they became available to a wider public. The availability of greater numbers of books meant that more people eventually learned to read and the society progressed as a whole.

Not too many years ago Christian educators and communicators were spreading the "gospel" of Super-8 film as a new and exciting method of teaching and communicating. Local churches and whole denominations spent a great deal of money, time, and effort to use this medium. Unfortunately, society was not willing to join the church in the use of this new medium even though it was relatively inexpensive (compared to 16-mm film). Its limitations in terms of film expense and nonreusability meant that it would never be widely used.

Even Eastman Kodak realized that Super-8 was about to go the way of the stereopticon when it announced that it would no longer make Super-8 movie cameras. Kodak and other manufacturers are predicting a complete camera/recorder the size of today's Super-8 movie camera within the next ten years.

It does not seem likely that the video format will be a "flash-in-the-pan" technology. Television has permeated our society unlike any medium in history. In the short period of time between 1950 and 1980, the population of TV sets in American homes has grown from 5 percent to 98.9 percent. In the next decade a majority of homes with a color TV (currently 80 percent of all homes with TV) will have some sort of videotape or video disc playback/record capability.

The use of magnetic tape to store and retrieve video images is a relatively new technology. The first videotape recorders were bulky (about the size of a refrigerator) and very expensive (several hundreds of thousands of dollars) and appeared in the 1960s. In the fifteen or so years since then, they have been reduced in size, price, and ease of use to the point where they are well within the reach of millions of homes. The development of the so-called home video recorder and its subsequent acceptance by the public have caused a revolution to begin—a revolution in the way Americans use television.

These new machines, which use a tape one-half inch wide encased in a cassette about the size of a paperback book, have sold at an unprecedented rate. There are already millions of them in use in homes today, and sales are increasing rapidly each year.

Marketed heavily during the Christmas buying season, these machines are advertised as a "time-shifting" device, a way to record a program broadcast at an inconvenient time for playback later. Another feature that is emphasized is the capability to record one program while showing another.

The growth in the production of prerecorded tapes for sale and video libraries has also been nothing short of phenomenal. It is now possible to buy, rent, or borrow hundreds of feature-length films, instructional tapes, and educational tapes for playback on these home units. Whole Bible study curricula are being designed and marketed. Programs originally seen on commercial TV are being marketed for the religious public.

Denominations and ecumenical organizations are developing programming for NBV. The Stewardship Committee of the National Council of Churches is working on a set of video resources on stewardship for the churches.

Color video cameras and portable recording equipment are now coming into the range of consumers as well, and the advertising is beginning to reflect the "home movie" capabilities of the equipment.

In short, video as a medium of communication, education, and entertainment is here to stay for a long time. A great deal of money is being invested by traditionally conservative businesses who are betting that American society will become increasingly dependent on video and other forms of electronic communication in the future.

Public schools are relying heavily on the new technology and will continue to do so in the future. The credibility of the churches' teaching ministry may be at stake when a student experiences lessons presented by teachers trained in the new technology and then is expected to take equally as seriously a lesson presented by a well-intentioned but more traditional style teacher.

This does not mean that all teachers should use TV or other media all the time. There is much to be said for the personal lesson by "example" that many church school teachers make. It is, however, going to be increasingly hard for those teachers to get the students' attention in an age when they are used to and feel comfortable with technologically supported teachers.

POSSIBLE USES OF NONBROADCAST VIDEO

There are many ways that NBV can be used in the life of the church. Let us look at some of them in relationship to the local church and regional and national church bodies.

NBV and the Local Church

The local congregation which owns or has access to video equipment is the unit of the church which stands to benefit most from its use. This is especially true if productions are done by members of the congregation. The possibilities seem to be limited only by the imagination of the people, but here are some suggestions.

1. Television can be used in leadership training. Just as videotape is now used in speech and homiletics classes, so it can be used in the church with church school teachers and other leaders. The minister can even use it to review and critique the leadership of worship and sermon delivery.

Think of the value of having videotape available so that the church school teachers can observe their own performance! In addition to this kind of use, there are also opportunities for training teachers and leaders through the use of tapes prepared by people with special skills. An expert in the use of denominational lesson materials or teaching methods can videotape a series of lessons for the teachers in local churches. These tapes could be made available through circulation by the denomination or by some other form of lending library.

2. Television can be used to preserve important moments in the life of the church. No one would ever excuse the failure to take pictures of a hundredth anniversary or the visit of a denominational leader or famous preacher. Videotape can be used to record these events, not only for viewing in subsequent years, but also for those who were not able to attend the event at the time it was held. When special events are recorded, people who were not able to attend can view them and still feel a part of the life of the congregation.

3. Worship services can be taped to share at a later date or can

even be broadcast by cable television in the local community. Also, just as cassette recordings have been used to share worship services with people who are homebound, so a videotape and player might be taken to the home by a visitor from the church. The service could then be played through the television set in the home.

4. There are many obvious advantages to the use of NBV in Christian education. Not only can it be used to bring special emphasis and information to the classroom in the church, but it can also be produced by students and shared with others. Another possibility is the development of material for use in the home. With NBV, a well-produced video series in conjunction with other media, and the help and example of the parents, a child will be able to receive much more than the hour or so of Christian education on Sunday morning. Another major area for growth lies in adult education. NBV can be used in the home so that busy adults will not have to schedule another meeting.

5. In addition to the areas of use already listed, there are a number of other uses of NBV that take advantage of the special features of the medium. Churches are becoming more aware of the educational needs of handicapped persons. NBV can help those with hearing losses by incorporating a "signer" in a small box in the corner of the screen or through a new technology called "tele-text" which allows for the encoding of special written messages or translations on the tape. These can be seen only on sets with a decoder, which means that one tape can be used with handicapped as well as nonhandicapped persons.

The language needs of minority groups in the church are also forcing the church to reexamine some of the ways it has been doing education. The dual-audio track capability of many of the new home recorders offers a solution to the problem of providing materials in two languages. One track can provide narration or dialogue in English and the other can be done in Spanish, for example. Simply by flipping a switch on the machine, either of the two languages can be heard.

A special message or presentation can be enhanced through video by the use of material recorded in specific locations. A documentary on the housing needs of a city or the degradation of life in the area of "sexploitation" will be far more effective than a monologue on the same subject. There is no end to what the imagination can conjure for the medium once it is in our hands to use.

NBV and Regional Religious Groups

One of the important functions of a regional church unit could be the administration of a video library and distribution center. Since churches in a given area tend to have similar characteristics and purposes, a prime use of the medium on this level might be to share ideas and information through video.

Presentations by missionaries and other resource persons who have a limited amount of time in a given area could be taped and then made available to a much larger number of churches in a region.

Not every church can have a football hero or a film personality or a singing sensation appear at its youth meetings. The state or regional office can encourage sessions where these people can be invited to tape their presentation so that youth throughout the region can share in the value of their appearance.

Standardization of equipment through a centralized purchasing plan might best work on a regional level as well. A planning team similar to those established for regional health plans might coordinate the purchase of equipment so that financial resources can be used efficiently. Just as hospitals in a given area decide together on which hospital will invest in very expensive pieces of equipment to avoid duplication, regional church units could coordinate video equipment purchases so that equipment bought by one church is compatible with that of other churches.

NBV National and International Applications

Large commercial companies are beginning to see the tremendous value of NBV for their operations. Company news and leadership training are being distributed on NBV at an ever-increasing rate. The savings in travel and related costs more than make up for the production costs. Upper level management can reach middle management and workers in a personal way not possible with other more traditional methods.

Denominational headquarters can make use of NBV in similar ways: offering appeals, curriculum resources, missionary interpretation (including actual scenes of the field), interpretation of denominational programs and emphases are all potential topics for NBV programming on a national level.

Existing film libraries can be transferred to video, reducing maintenance costs and providing an even wider market, since the tapes can be rented to individuals who want to view them for their own edification or inspiration and can be shown on one's own TV at home. Very few individuals own 16-mm film projectors; yet if the projections for future home video machines are correct, many church members will have the capability of replaying this type of programming within the next five to ten years.

NONBROADCAST VIDEO AND OTHER MEDIA

One of the first lessons a communicator must learn is the selection of the proper, most efficient way of imparting the message to the listener/viewer. Each medium, whether it is print, film, slides, records, sermons, or video, must be selected on its own merits for the job that needs to be done.

Nonbroadcast video does offer several advantages over other forms of media traditionally used in a church setting. NBV is considerably easier to use by unskilled persons. Anyone who can use a standard audio cassette recorder can use a video recorder to play back prerecorded materials. Video does not require a darkened room or a screen. Everything can be loaded onto a cart and simply rolled into a room and plugged in. Press two buttons, and the show begins. There is no film to break, no bulbs to replace. The machines themselves are very reliable and have a low rate of repair. Tapes can be stopped at any point, rewound, and played again to emphasize or clarify a point. While this can be done with film, filmstrips, or slides, the process is time-consuming and often is not done because of the inconvenience. NBV, then, offers a good chance to use the effective "programmed learning" technique in a teaching/learning situation.

Because videotape can be duplicated easily and rapidly, there is no need to produce an expensive inventory of tapes that may or may not be used. Libraries need only store one master and then copy it to send to users. Since videotape can be reused, unlike film, libraries can send out a program on one tape, erase it when it returns, and use the tape over again for an entirely different program.

For those who want to do their own production, NBV offers the advantage of being able to see the finished product immediately without having to wait for film processing. With automatic cameras a well-exposed picture is almost guaranteed.

NBV is primarily designed for small group or individual use. Film would be more suitable for presentation of resources to a larger group, such as a congregation, unless one is willing to spend several thousand dollars on a large screen video projector or many TV sets placed around the room. Overhead projection would be a better medium if the instructor is going to personalize the lesson with other information or write during the course of the lesson. Slides can be used when an illustration or two are all that are needed. Flannelgraphs might be a way to involve the students better in the telling of a story, although many young children are very adept at the use of video as a means of expression.

Whatever the communications objective, NBV gets the word (and picture) across in a familiar, contemporary medium. While it can be argued that many of these applications can be achieved through the use of other media, the ease of use and production makes video a logical choice for use in the church.

The Advantages of Television

This chapter will describe some of the advantages and limitations of television as a tool for communication within the church and church family (including the denomination). The newness of the medium for *nonbroadcast* applications causes some to fear it, believing that the use of television requires technical expertise and a special talent for electronics. But, in fact, it will take no more expertise to use the technology of television than it took to learn to do a good job on the mimeograph. Indeed, it is entirely possible that the videotape recorder will become as commonplace in the church as the mimeograph is today.

WHAT IS TELEVISION?

It might seem terribly academic to try to define television. Television is hardly one of the unknowns of our generation. But it is precisely because it is so well known that time should be taken to define it. Since, as you will see, the word "television" can have a number of meanings, it is important that we agree on its meaning for the purpose of our discussion. This seemingly simple exercise may become as difficult as a fish trying to define water.

We use the word "television" in a number of ways. First, television is that modern invention by which picture and sound are transmitted via radio waves from a point of origin to a receiver. For most of us this would be the basic and first definition. Some of us can remember when broadcasting was done without pictures—when radio was more than spinning records and reading news. The technology for changing picture information into electronic impulses was invented in the late 1920s and became commercially available after World War II. At first the technology was crude. The early television cameras were large and heavy. Videotape was developed late in the game; so all early video broadcasting had to be done live. In these early years, broadcast television was all we could think about. There was no technology for the nonbroadcast use of the new medium.

Second, when we say "television," we mean any use of the video camera and television receiver to create picture information. Thus we have television in banks to monitor customer behavior; we have television in elevators for surveillance of the passengers; we have television in classrooms to monitor performance.

Third, television is the content of the broadcast medium. When Newton Minnow coined his phrase, "Television is a vast waste land," he used the word "television" in this way. He was not talking about the transmission and reception of picture and sound; he was referring to the content of those pictures and sounds. Often when we speak about "television," we mean not the medium but the content of the medium.

Fourth, television is an industry. If we were to say, "Television employs thousands of people," we would be referring neither to the camera and receiver nor to the program content but to the industry that uses and exploits both.

This variety of uses of the word "television" may be confusing as the discussion shifts back and forth from television as the program content to television as the recording and reproduction of picture and sound. In this chapter and the next two, however, "television" will be primarily used to refer to the taking, recording, and reproducing of pictures and sound.

SPECIAL USES AND LIMITATIONS OF TELEVISION

With all the wonders ascribed to the new medium of television, one might think that it can do everything. But there are some things it cannot do. There are some things it can do but ought not to do. There are some things it can do but which other media can do better.

Once a friend and I were planning to have dinner together. I said that I would like to be home by nine o'clock because there was a program on television I wanted to see. Her reply—mostly in jest—was "I would never let television govern my life!" This represents one of the primary hindrances to the use of television in the church: the idea that television is a time-waster, low-grade entertainment for the uncultured, never to be taken seriously. I asked my friend, "Would you let your intention to go to the movies govern the time you spent at dinner? Or, if you had a season ticket to the theater, would that schedule limit your acceptance of other social engagements?" Of course, the answers were obvious. But the universal reaction seems to be, "But that's different!"

There is still a kind of intellectual snobbery with regard to television that relegates all of it to the realm of the comic book. Many of my colleagues boast, "I never watch television." This is said to support somehow their intellectual superiority to those of us who do. Douglass Cater puts it this way: "The thinking person is apt to be somewhat bewildered by the telly and to regard it in the same way a back-sliding prohibitionist regards hard liquor—as something to be indulged in with a sense of guilt."[1] Churches and church people will resist the use of television in the church because it seems to them that the instrument is used for wasting time in useless pleasure. Church people and intellectuals are not alone in this opinion. Schools and parents have often fostered the notion that the television is something to be avoided until all else is finished, and the best of our culture has been exhausted. Yet, in spite of these attitudes, Cater points out that "the educated viewer . . . even when he had a clear choice between an information program and some standard entertainment fare . . . was just as apt as other to choose the latter."[2] To overcome this limitation, we will have to exercise skill in demonstrating the value of the medium, and we will have to allow time for our puritanical values to subside.

A second limitation on the use of television is that people confronted with a television set expect to be entertained. The vast majority of material on television is purely for entertainment. Not even entertainment is without some social, attitudinal, and value orientation, however. Public service, news, and informational programming are now concentrating their production techniques on making information programs also entertaining.

It will be the same when the church begins producing television

[1]Douglass Cater and Richard Adler, eds., *Television as a Social Force: New Approaches to TV Criticism* (New York: Praeger Publishers, 1975), p. 2.
[2]*Ibid.*

programs. All of us—not only our children and youth—are living in an environment of quality production of entertainment. As a result, local amateur productions are not well received. Even the remotest congregation is exposed to a constant barrage of excellence in television production.

The churches will have to move in two directions to encourage the use of nonbroadcast television in the church. First, we will have to change the expectancy of the viewer. Though we might do everything our skills and funds permit to make our productions entertaining and skillfully produced, our purpose is not to entertain nor to win awards for excellence in production; our purpose is to communicate. I am convinced that the continued use of the nonbroadcast medium will in time alter viewer expectancy. Second, we will have to encourage the development of video productions that are as professional as we can make them. We should never let our quality become just "good enough" for our own people. We can do no less than to sharpen all of the creative skills we have to do the job right.

A third limitation is that television cannot do everything. We tend to think that an investment in the equipment for television production and reproduction demands that it replace all of the audiovisual and communications tools we have been using. But television, for instance, cannot answer questions from the audience. A taped performer cannot give immediate response—only the speaker who comes in person can do that.

Each medium has strengths and weaknesses. Most of this book will be extolling the strengths of television. It is important, therefore, that we also mention some of the weaknesses.

First there is the question of *resolution*. The Federal Communications Commission in 1941 authorized television broadcasting at the current engineering standards. From then on the standard television for broadcasting would consist of a dot of light that scans 525 lines thirty times each second. Because of the complexity of television electronics, we seem to be locked into that level of picture resolution. For most applications the resolution of the American system is adequate. However, a 2″ x 2″ slide can give far better resolution than the TV picture tube. To use a slide on TV is to reduce both the size and the detail of the slide.

Second, there is the "smaller-than-life" aspect of the television screen. It is convenient to have movies shown on television so the viewer does not have to leave home. However, film tends to make things bigger than life. It is almost laughable to see a Cecil B. DeMille spectacular with its vast backgrounds shown on a screen no larger than twenty by fifteen inches. When it is important to give a bigger-than-life feeling, film is superior to television.

Third, television allows for—in fact, encourages—distractions. It is not used in a darkened room. Therefore, other items, other people, other happenings distract the viewer. Our usual habit with television in the home is to turn away from the program for comment and conversation whenever we feel the urge to do so.

Fourth, television can never be as effective as a live person, especially if the same person who could appear in person is shown, instead, on tape. I once worked with some high school teachers who had been given access to some rather sophisticated video equipment. They wanted me to help them determine how they ought to use it. After going through some of the advantages of video, I asked that they come prepared the next time to recommend specific kinds of lessons for videotaping. Nearly all of them came prepared to do what they knew best: They would lecture, using such visuals as chalkboard and maps on the wall. When I asked where the teacher would be while the students watched the television, the answer was, "In the classroom, prepared to answer questions and conduct discussion." They were able to ask the next obvious question: "Why go to the trouble and expense of putting onto videotape what would be more effective done live?" There may be good reason to duplicate a classroom situation on broadcast television (for example, "Sunrise Semester"), but there is little reason to duplicate the classroom on tape to be used in the classroom.

Each medium has its own advantage. To study detail over a sustained period of time, no picture medium is better than the slide. To develop progressive thought where errors must be corrected and constant change is required, nothing is better than the chalkboard. To unfold information progressively, the best medium is the overhead projector. For the teacher who uses these media but wants to preserve a specific lecture for other classes for which the teacher cannot or should not be present, these media can be taped with the lecture.

It is important to remember that while television has many uses, one ought not use it to the exclusion of other media simply because it is available and popular.

TELEVISION AS AN IMMEDIATE MEDIUM

Until videotape was made available at a reasonably low price, audio-visuals used at the church or school had to be made by photographic methods; that is, the process required a camera and a film that had to be developed. This technique meant that there was a significant time lapse between the event and the replay. With the development of magnetic recording, this process began to change.

I remember that when I took a speech class in college, only one of our speeches was recorded. The recording was made on a wax disc into which a sound groove was cut by the recording needle. This was the same basic recorder we had used in junior high school to record the WPA Symphony Orchestra concerts and other events at the school. Before the end of my college career we were making use of the wire recorder (grandfather to present tape recorders). Convenient sound monitoring became a reality with the wire recorder. Speech classes no longer needed to depend on the unwieldy and expensive wax disc recording. The convenience of the magnetic recording age had begun.

With videotape, the same convenience we have had for sound is now available for sight. Speakers, teachers, or performers can have their performance recorded and played back for immediate feedback and evaluation. No development time, no processing—just as quickly as one can find the place on the tape, the tape can be replayed.

Videotape, then, is the most usable, flexible, and inexpensive tool for feedback we have. Even though the initial expense for equipment for 35-mm and Super-8 film is considerably less than the capital investment required in video equipment, the film stock is far more expensive. Film cannot be reused; it can be duplicated only at considerable expense and delay.

Videotape is used as a matter of course to monitor performance in such classes as public speaking, preaching, musical conducting, practice teaching, and especially teaching the handicapped. The church and church organizations would derive the same benefits from this constant monitoring of performance as the schools have experienced.

A constant plea among church school teachers is for more teacher training. What better training could there be than to monitor a given performance and, with experts and peers, evaluate and suggest ways to overcome problems? Though it is often painful, preachers can benefit from watching and listening to their sermons—in all the same ways the congregation did—by using videotape.

We often teach by group methods. Wouldn't we get a better grasp of our goal attainment if we were to videotape group sessions and play them back to see if we did what we set out to do? It is so difficult to be within the group and try at the same time to evaluate the dynamics of the group.

Sharing groups can be videotaped. This would require a very special group with some very cautious restraints on the use of the tape. Self-evaluation of one's own performance in a group like this would be of extreme value.

Even more valuable would be the taping of administrative groups. How often do we get a chance to see directly the dynamics of our boards and committees? If the deliberations were videotaped and played back, then each committee could get the feel for how they advance or impede the progress toward goals. It boggles the mind to imagine what would happen in the hallowed halls of denominational deliberations if administrators were subjected to instant replay of their words and deeds!

Because of the small operating expense, videotape can be used to preserve nearly all of the important events that a church or group may experience. The instant-replay discs used so effectively in sporting events actually record only a few seconds of play. They keep recording over and over, erasing what happened before, until the director calls for a play to be repeated. Then the machine retains the twenty seconds or so that are to be replayed. If it is spectacular enough to be saved for the recap, the disc is removed and replaced. If it is so spectacular that it should be reserved for the archives, it can be kept permanently.

In a similar way all, or nearly all, of the events at a church, region, or state could be recorded on videotape. That which proves worth keeping can be kept. Because the tape is reusable, the same tape, if not kept, can be used for the next recording. Thus, unimportant events can be recorded and discarded, and important events are never missed.

The kinds of events that one might later wish to revisit would include a very special service at the church, an anniversary celebration, a favorite pastor's last sermon, a guest preacher who did a spectacular job. These are the once-in-a-lifetime kinds of programs that become nothing but memory without some kind of recording. Just think! Would you let Billy Graham speak in your church and expect no one to take pictures? Years ago there were undoubtedly events about which, even now, someone will take out the pictures and reminisce.

Television has been able to bring contemporary history into our living rooms as it was being made: the Kennedy assassination, the Vietnam War, the Watergate events, the Army-McCarthy hearings are taught as strange events in recent history. The replay of the tapes causes us to *relive* that frightening time. Videotape can cause us to relive the good and the bad, the fondly remembered and the long forgotten.

We often want to record special dramatic events. If our children or youth are giving a performance, we would want, of course, to preserve it forever. However, two cautions must be offered along with the encouragement to do so.

First, staging an event for presentation to an audience and staging it for television cameras require two different techniques. We have learned to live with live presentation of opera and ballet on television because it allows us to recall what it was like to be there in the theater. It is significant that those who have never been to the opera don't care to watch it on television. When we record a dramatic performance, the playback is subconsciously compared with the dramas (especially the soap operas) we have seen on TV. And because the performance was not organized (blocked) for the camera, we are disappointed, and we either blame the inadequate equipment or amateur operators or excuse the production because, after all, the performers were just children. The fact is, a performance can be done well by amateurs if they prepare the performance with the camera in mind and forget their ideas about play acting for an audience.

The second caution is that church groups can get away with using material, under certain circumstances, that would normally require the payment of royalties. If your group is performing a play without consideration of the fee—perhaps they didn't know there should have been a fee!—putting it onto videotape for others to see could raise a legal question. So, if you are to tape a performance—even a musical performance—be aware of the licensing and royalty arrangement with the author, composer, and publisher (who are usually represented by a group like ASCAP).

There are numerous books and articles that can help the interested amateur prepare the camera work and staging for using television for dramatics. (See Appendix 2.)

There are times when a group of churches—such as those in a specific region or state convention—could afford to use the services of an expert in some aspect of our church life. We try to get everyone concerned to attend the sessions with the experts, but how often have we later remarked, "If only so-and-so had been at that session!" Videotape can preserve that event in such a way that expertise can be shared over a longer period of time with a greater number of people. This sharing can even be accomplished in the fellowship of the local church—around the church TV set—or in a family's home.

Using videotape to get wider exposure of experts dovetails with our emphasis on using television to bring people into a close relationship with the audience. The "expert" is no longer an abstraction at the front of a long auditorium; the "expert" is right here with us. This same value can be exploited in missionary promotion. It was a great help when missionaries could bring back slides of their work—it would be even better if more of them were trained to use them well! But to have the missionary talk to us while he or she is still in the field, still doing the work, bringing us directly into that situation, or better, bringing that situation right into our own parlor—think of the effect that would have on making missions personal.

The immediacy of the medium can be exploited in such simple areas as showing specific kinds of materials and how they are to be used. Rather than having copies of books, pamphlets, or reproductions of pages from these materials, video can focus in on these items and make them available to all while the leader calls attention to specifics. To do this with other media, while less expensive if videotape is not readily available, is cumbersome and time consuming and requires expert advanced planning. One could use the opaque projector to display printed materials, but the opaque projector is extremely heavy and is not in general use. It might be difficult even to find one to borrow. Overhead transparencies could be prepared—this would be the recommended course if the investment had not already been made in video—but this requires advanced planning to see that the transparencies are actually produced. Thirty-five-millimeter slides could be made of the materials to be read. This is effective but less effective than the overhead projector. It would not be practical to bring video into a session simply to amplify the visuals for all to see, but, if the session is being preserved on video, this medium has the capacity to preserve also the specific visuals and printed information without actual copies accompanying the presentation.

3

Using the Intimacy of Television

In spite of the push toward big-screen television, our usual acquaintance with television is through the set in our home. It is a relatively small box, often situated in the room in such a way as to permit us to walk around it. We can pick it up and move it. It sits in our living room, talks to us while we eat, shares those last moments before we go to sleep, and often becomes our first contact with the world when we awake in the morning.

TELEVISION AS AN INTIMATE MEDIUM

Three aspects of television contribute to its intimacy: (1) the presence of the set and its contents (programming) in our home, (2) the small size of the screen and its limited resolution, (3) the economics of the television industry in its infancy which dictated the use of limited settings.

The limitations of screen size and resolution, described in chapter 2, also create some of the uniqueness of television. It would be difficult to get the "cast of thousands" effect of a DeMille movie on a screen that measures twenty-five inches on the diagonal. It would be hard to get a feeling for the height of the Colossus while looking down on the TV picture. In most of our homes the TV set is situated in such a way that the top of the set is below eye level even while we are seated.

This small screen does lend itself well to picturing people. A twenty-five-inch diagonal screen is actually twenty inches across and fifteen inches high. If a grown person (approximately seventy-two inches high) were shown full length (called a long-shot) on a twenty-five-inch set placed eight feet from the viewer, the person would appear to be thirty-eight feet away. But on the other hand, a picture of just the person's face (called an *ECU* or *extreme close-up*) would appear to be closer than the set itself. (See Glossary for definitions of italicized terms.) The smaller the set, the farther away each of the long-shots will appear to be. Because we know that most people watch on small screens (twelve to seventeen inches diagonal) we tend to prefer closeup shots. This practice has made television an intimate medium.

Even if the television industry in its infancy had not discovered that the illusion of closeness is created by concentrating on people, especially people close up, they would have created intimacy anyway. Television broadcasting began before videotaping was invented and before there were successful ways to use film. Programs had to be produced live with live transitions from setting to setting. Television drama could not call on vast outdoor sets intermixed with indoor settings. All of the sets had to be within rolling distance of studio cameras and, therefore, on the same stage in order to be sequenced without significant breaks. Consequently, early television concentrated on people, their faces, reactions, and interactions. This, too, established television as an intimate medium.

No matter what program content we use, no matter to what purpose we put our television programming, we will not be able to erase the idea that television is the instrument through which newspersons, performers, and public figures have entered our home. Horace Newcomb suggests in *TV: The Most Popular Art* that this can be seen best in the difference between the television Western and the movie Western. "In the Western movie, panorama, movement, and environment are crucial to the very idea of the West. . . . On television this sense of expansiveness is meaningless."[1] He further suggests that television is at its best when it offers reactions to the action rather than simply the action itself.

Nothing in television production is more often criticized than the "talking head," a picture of a person talking and nothing more. Never-

[1]Horace Newcomb, *TV: The Most Popular Art* (Garden City, N.Y.: Anchor Press/ Doubleday, 1974), p.248.

theless, in professional television the "talking head" is a common phenomenon. News programs are comprised largely of the newsperson on camera, talking. Discussion programs are a sequence of "talking heads." It would be a mistake to think that every person who appears talking on camera is an instance of the dreaded "talking head." There are a number of reasons to seek creative ways to use the "talking head." Not the least of these is to create intimacy. Let's take a look at how to achieve intimacy.

Most newsletters and "in-house" periodicals include a warm greeting from the chief administrative officer of the organization. Through this he or she attempts to speak directly and personally to the reader. The style of these can range from a signed column in *Newsweek* to an editorial in the *New York Times*. But except for those few who know the author personally, these editorials seldom take on the person-to-person character of a word from Howard K. Smith or Walter Cronkite.

What if the pastor, executive minister, area minister—or bishop, district superintendent, etc.—were to talk directly to the viewer through television? What if you could read the feeling in the person's face, the anguish in the eyes, the sincerity in one's manner? Is it possible that more Baptists feel they know Walter Cronkite than know the general secretary of the American Baptist Churches? Do more Catholics know Dan Rather than know any of the American cardinals? Do more Episcopalians know William Buckley than know the presiding bishop? Probably so. This is a direct result of the intimacy of television. Those who have appeared on television have been in our homes.

Church newsletters, and especially the pastor's column, are sometimes informative, theological, folksy, but seldom personal or intimate. Intimate use of television calls for a "talking head" with some cautions. Intimacy involves people speaking to or communicating with people, and a number of varieties of the "talking head" can help us develop this sense of intimacy.

PROGRAMMING WITH A SINGLE PERFORMER

The most problematic use of a single performer, a "talking head," is that which includes no other visual. That is, there are no *graphics*, illustrations, pictures, inserts, other people for response and/or reaction shots. (See Glossary for definitions of italicized terms.) While this format has received just criticism, it would be foolish to dismiss as totally unacceptable any use of a single person talking directly to a viewer.

A person making a speech to an audience is not talking directly to the viewer but to the live audience. The viewer is a secondary recipient. The viewer may, in fact, feel closer to the speaker than do those present in the hall, but we cannot create the illusion that the speaker is speaking to the viewer alone. In a situation of this kind the viewer ought to be given the chance to look around at the audience for their reaction because this is what one might do if he or she were present in the hall.

A speaker speaks to the viewer only when the eye contact with the viewer is singular, as it would be in conversation. News commentary is a prime example of this. The comment is directed toward the viewer and no one else. The commentator looks directly into the camera—which in turn makes him or her look directly out of the TV set into the eyes of the viewer. Gerald Millerson in his book. *Effective TV Production*, suggests that "no other production format provides such close communication with the audience as the single performer— nor a bigger bore if the presentation is inept."[2]

Let's take a look at two forms of the single performer for some clues to good production using the "talking head."

The single performer without visuals

The performer is on his or her own. This format has been sanctified on radio through the "fireside chats" of Franklin Delano Roosevelt. It has been used effectively by such pioneers as Lowell Thomas and Elmer Davis and was perfected by the skills of Edward R. Murrow. It is still being used effectively on radio by Paul Harvey and others.

Television adds a dimension to the single talking performer that radio does not have. Not only must the television performer develop a skillful sequence of words and deliver them with power, but television demands that the performer also express himself or herself through such nonverbal factors as facial expression, body position, posture, camera angle, and apparent proximity.

The single performer will most often appear on a single camera. Multiple cameras can provide relief from the monotony of a single point of view, but they are difficult to use well. Even professionals who use the technique of multiple cameras often make it seem awkward. Alistair Cooke in his introductions to "Masterpiece Theater" (PBS) is often reoriented to a different camera during his talk. The shift appears

---

[2] Gerald Millerson, *Effective TV Production* (New York: Hastings House Publishers, 1976), p. 156.

strained and unnatural. For beginners the single camera for the single performer is preferable. Shift in emphasis can be accomplished by changing the apparent distance of the speaker from the viewer by using the *zoom lens*. When the speaker is speaking in generalities, giving background, setting the issue in perspective, the camera will view the speaker as if from a greater distance, but as the speaker becomes personal, intimate, animated, then the camera brings the speaker closer. One way to get a feel for these changes is to observe people in a one-to-one conversation. When does the speaker lean forward to the listener, and when does he or she tend to back away from that intimacy? The single camera using the zoom lens can establish an intimate relationship between the speaker and the viewer.

A single camera can also communicate messages along with the words of the speaker through the camera angle. Students on a college campus were asked to observe the camera work of a TV crew during a student demonstration. They reported predictably that when the students were being interviewed, the cameras were held high looking down on the interviewee; when administration personnel were being interviewed, the camera was held at eye level or below. The effect was to make the students look petty and to make the administration appear powerful and in charge. But one angle is not always negative and the other positive. For example, if the speaker wishes to appear humble or pleading, he would recommend a high camera angle. To appear powerful, in control, the speaker would suggest a low camera angle.

To achieve the effect of intimacy with the "talking head," preparation is important. The speaker's delivery must be as though he or she were speaking to a single person; yet he or she must be prepared to speak without hesitation. If his or her speech sounds memorized, it will lose its personal character. If it is spoken hesitantly, it will lose its authority. If it appears to be read, it will lose its credibility.

If speakers have stage experience, they may be able to deliver memorized lines convincingly. If they are not accomplished public speakers used to memorizing speeches, they will probably not deliver memorized lines as if they were one-to-one conversation.

If the speaker reads the message, he or she must convince the viewer that the message is not being read. If that is not possible—and in some cases, like reading the news, it is not desirable—the speaker must convince the viewer that he or she is reading it for just that individual.

The speaker must not be distracted by the presence of camera and crew. The illusion of intimacy can be destroyed when the speaker glances at a *monitor, floor director,* or other technical distractions. However, people do not like continuous uninterrupted eye contact. In some of your conversations note how often you will glance away from the person with whom you are talking. For an experiment sometime— and I recommend this only with a good friend—try prolonged conversation without ever taking your eyes off the eyes of your companion. Then you will realize the importance of relief from direct eye contact. If, however, when you take your eyes off your companion, you appear to be looking at someone or something else, your companion's eyes will try to find what you are seeing. Since this situation can lead to extreme frustration if your companion is at home and you are in the studio, your glance away from eye contact ought to be at nothing in particular—down at your hands, up over the camera, just the way you would do in face-to-face conversation.

How, then, can the speaker be sure to present the information the way he or she planned and still maintain intimacy?

First, through memorization—this, as I have suggested, is recommended only for the performer who is absolutely sure of his or her proficiency.

Second, by the use of a teleprompter—this is a mechanical or electronic device available in a variety of models. It is very helpful but too expensive for the small producer. Homemade versions of the teleprompter can be developed by skillful tinkers. A device that can turn a roll of paper at the proper speed can be placed just above or just below the camera. Large print—large enough to be read at the distance the speaker is from the camera—is printed on the roll. The roll is then turned, either mechanically or by hand, as the speaker reads. Another simple form of teleprompter uses a regular, or slightly larger, form of typewriter. The speech is typed on a roll. The rolling type passes in front of the lens of a small video camera. The video signal is fed to a large monitor placed just above or just below the camera into which the speaker is speaking. The speaker reads the print from the monitor. A special advantage of this video teleprompter is that the signal can be sent to a number of monitors placed at separate cameras for multiple-camera programming. The contemporary professional method is to use a glass in front of the camera lens and to project the printed speech onto the glass. It is not registered in the camera but allows the speaker to read as he or she looks directly into the lens. This is very handy but quite expensive.

Third, the "idiot card" is less expensive and less taxing on the creativity of your studio planner. This consists of a series of cards large enough to include whole paragraphs of the text but small enough to be handled easily by the *floor director*. There are typewriterlike printers for "idiot cards," but a felt-tip pen printing legibly is adequate for the task. The cards should be held as close to the camera lens as possible without being caught on camera.

Fourth, some professionals make use of the audio cassette recorder. This method would be distracting for the beginner. Some news commentators record their speech on audio cassette, place the "hearing aid"-type earphone in their ears, and repeat on camera what they are whispering to themselves in the ear.

Fifth, notes and reminders, rather than complete texts, can be used with any of the above methods. An experienced and confident speaker can use the notes to keep an even, personal flow of ideas.

With proper attention to the use of the camera, with adequate preparation and prompting, and with an awareness of nonverbal language, the "talking head," without any added support, can be legitimate and effective.

The single performer with visuals

When only one person is speaking but has something to show, the "talking head" takes on new dimensions. The process affords new dimensions. The process affords new opportunities and new problems for the production team. There are a number of ways to approach this situation. The way you choose will depend on your skills as a producer and the sophistication of your equipment.

First, to use a single camera technique without the benefit of proper *editing equipment* will require careful planning and placement of your visuals. *Panning* a live camera from the "talking head" to the visual can be effective if it is used sparingly. Excessive or too rapid panning can leave the viewer with motion sickness. An effective alternative to the direct pan is a zoom-pan combination. You will zoom out, keeping the speaker at one edge of the picture until the picture includes both the speaker and the visual. You can reverse the process to lose the visual and pick up the speaker again. With practice this technique can be very effective.

The single-camera technique makes it difficult to switch from the objective point of view (the viewer seeing the speaker and visual from his or her viewing angle) to the subjective point of view (the viewer seeing the visual from the viewing angle of the speaker). To do this with the single camera requires editing equipment.

Visuals made specifically for use on television can be made to fit the dimensions of the TV screen. Visuals that are made for another medium—slides, for example—must be adapted for television. The TV screen is 3 units high and 4 units wide, making the diagonal 5 units in length. Remember high school geometry, especially the formula for triangles: $a^2 + b^2 = c^2$? Hence, whenever you make visuals, make sure they fit the 3:4 ratio *(aspect ratio)* of television. You also ought to be aware of the focusing limitations of your camera. Don't prepare visuals so small that the camera cannot get in close enough to focus. Many of the books listed in Appendix 2 deal extensively with the production of graphics. They are highly recommended.

A second technique using the single camera adds the editing function. This is often referred to as the "film" technique. Using this technique, you will take the program in bits and then piece them together. Every time a new camera angle is called for, you will stop the tape, reorient the camera, then shoot the next scene. Meanwhile, back at the production bench, the various shots will be intercut into proper sequence. This allows for changes of location. In one documentary John Kenneth Galbraith was able to deliver a smoothly flowing lecture while appearing at locations in far separate countries without apparent interruption. The development of sophisticated, yet relatively inexpensive, editing capability for videotape gives video a flexibility once reserved for film.

PROGRAMMING WITH INTERVIEWS OR PANELS

So far we have been talking about the single speaker "talking head" who is directing the message toward the individual viewer as audience (receiver). Other forms of the "talking head" are directed toward on-the-set receivers, while the viewer is a third party looking on. These formats include the interview, the conversation, the panel discussion, etc. While persons on the set may establish occasional eye contact with the audience and address occasional remarks to the camera, they do so for special effect and not as a usual procedure. I recall watching a political ad on TV in which one person posed as a reporter to ask the candidate a question. The candidate, rather than answering the reporter, turned to the camera and talked directly to the viewer. The result was an uncomfortable mixture of techniques.

The interview is different from conversation in that an interview is usually more purposeful. It differs from the formal question-and-answer format in that both parties speak and both listen. The serious purpose can take a wide variety of forms. For our purposes here the interviewer will either elicit pertinent information from the person who has the information or will offer the guest the opportunity to unfold his or her personality.

Certain techniques enhance one's ability as an interviewer. The interviewer should remember that he or she is the representative of the viewer and, as such, asks questions the viewer would ask if it were possible. There is no need for the interviewer to show how much he or she knows about the subject or about the guest, but the interviewer should not play dumb either! If an interviewer engages in "inside jokes" and exchanges private conversation, the viewer will feel left out. Remember, as an interviewer you are the go-between for the viewer and the guest.

The combination of an inexperienced interviewer and a nervous guest might lead to a series of closed questions with short, dull answers. For example:

INTERVIEWER: I understand you took a trip to Haiti.
GUEST: Yes.
INTERVIEWER: Were your shocked by the poverty there?
GUEST: No.
INTERVIEWER: Was it just as you expected?
GUEST: Just about. . . .

And so the interview would continue for as long as the program lasted. A more appropriate set of questions are what can be called "open questions":

What mission fields have you visited?
What did you discover there
How did that affect you? etc.

The mirror question is a tool for getting the guest to elaborate on an answer or to clarify an answer without letting him or her know it was unclear. For example: "You say the poverty was just as you expected?" Then the guest would feel free to elaborate on what it was he or she expected.

Probing questions, like the mirror question, call for the guest to go into more depth. This is the kind of question that sounds so harsh and abrupt when Mike Wallace uses it, but it can be handled more gently. Questions like "How?" and "Why?", for example, call for explanations and depth. A simple "uh-huh" or "I see" would offer the same opportunity.

Leading questions can help the guest get to a specific point he or she wants to make, for example, "Weren't you thrilled with the work of our missionaries there?" But the leading question should be used with great caution. If used to manipulate the guest, it will create a negative reaction in both the guest and the viewer.

Some interviewers forget that in the definition of an interview we find the suggestion that both people listen! Occasionally an interviewer will have a sequence of questions which he or she attempts to follow even though the next question is made redundant by the previous answer. It is proper to prepare questions, but let the sequence flow as the theme develops. Don't be afraid to follow up on answers with questions you don't have on your list.

An interview can use the single-camera setup. The single camera without editing will often concentrate on the guest, offering the viewer a subjective point of view, as though the viewer were also the interviewer looking the guest in the eye. If the objective point of view is desirable, the one camera can be operated to accomplish this and still avoid the monotony of a continuous *two-shot*. For example, let the camera open with an *establishing* two-shot of the interviewer and the guest while the interviewer introduces the guest. As the guest begins to answer the first question, zoom the camera in to a *one-shot* of the guest. Hold a one-shot of the guest for his or her reaction to the next question. When it seems that the guest is near the end of the answer, zoom back to the two-shot; then zoom immediately to the interviewer for the next question. Be cautious, however, because the zoom can have the same effect as the pan in causing motion sickness in the viewer.

Where editing is possible, the single camera can be used more effectively. While the interviewer asks the questions and the guest answers, keep the camera on the guest. After the complete interview, keep the people in place. Move the camera to an over-the-shoulder shot of the interviewer. Let the interviewer ask the questions again—without answers this time. These questions can then be intercut into the final tape.

The interview program is enhanced if it can take place in a studio with multiple cameras and *switching* capability. The switching should be rational; that is, the camera angle should change at the exact moment the viewer would probably have changed his or her viewing perspective if he or she had been in the audience. Knowing when to switch comes with practice and observation.

Careful use of microphones is as important as the use of the camera. The most comfortable way to use microphones is for each person to have a microphone. *Lavalieres* (neck mikes) are the best, especially if the guest is not accustomed to using a microphone. Microphones on a stand tend to keep inexperienced people leaning into the mike. They also tend to keep the participants aware of the presence of the mike. The lavaliere, on the other hand, is soon forgotten.

If a single microphone is used, it is important that the interviewer keep it in his or her own hands. He or she controls the interview, symbolically and practically, through possession of the mike. When the interviewer moves the microphone gently away from the guest, the guest knows the answer has been terminated.

A gentle movement of the microphone (in an upright position with the business end facing upward) back and forth just below the chins of guest and interviewer is less threatening than a mike pointed directly into the face of the guest.

The conversation, while utilizing the same camera and microphone techniques, is different from the interview in that there need not be a preconceived serious purpose to the conversation. Dick Cavett and Johnny Carson are more conversationalists than interviewers; Mike Wallace is an interviewer.

Before leaving the topic of the "talking head," let's talk briefly about multiple-person programming. There are a number of variations on this format: the one-on-many as in the "David Susskind Show"; many-on-one as in "Meet the Press"; one-among-many as in the year-end roundup of some network news teams.

Through all of this runs a common thread. The picture is always of a person talking, a person with whom the viewer is offered an intimate relationship. And as a result, the viewer is drawn into the picture as an active participant.

In a play on the BBC some time ago, the camera *trucks* along a series of storefronts until it spots a couple seated inside a restaurant. The camera (that is, the viewer) stays outside the window looking in toward the couple enjoying intimate conversation. At the man's request, a waiter comes to close the drapes, thus shutting the viewer out. At that point the viewer becomes aware that he or she has been drawn into the action. This is intimacy of the television medium.

4

The Production of Videotape

One of the advantages of using videotape is the ease with which videotape can be reproduced. Film requires laboratory treatment for reproduction, and the process is very expensive. Videotape can be reproduced by the user using unsophisticated equipment. You can, therefore, have all of the advantages of film without the high cost of film reproduction, storage, and distribution. Let's take a look at how these advantages work.

First, videotape is reusable. If you or your organization wants to make more than one copy of a program, you may *dub* as many copies as are needed. When the copies are no longer needed, they can be erased and the tape used for other projects. Experience has shown that you will need more copies of a program just after the program has been produced. Demand dwindles as time passes. During the high demand period, you can make copies from your original. When there is no longer a demand, the only copy you might want to keep is the original. The rest can be erased and used for future projects. Each tape can be used hundreds of times, depending on the quality of the tape and the care given to the tape in use. Film, on the other hand, can be used only once. Film copies are permanent and cannot be erased or reused.

Second, videotape is inexpensive. An hour's worth of tape costs between twenty and twenty-five dollars—depending on the quality and format. Nothing is lost in the editing process; edits are made by putting the sequences on a second tape in the order desired. Neither the original nor the edited copy is cut or destroyed. Any tape that contains material you don't want to use in the final edited copy can simply be erased for future use. Because no tape is lost in the editing process, the cost of tape for the edited program is no more than the cost per hour of raw tape. Film, on the other hand, carries the cost of all the film used: the original raw footage plus each copy. Assuming that you shoot four times as much material as you will use in the finished program, let us compare the cost of Super-8 film to the cost of videotape. (Sixteen-millimeter film is considerably more expensive and uses more expensive equipment; 35-mm movie film is out of the question for the small producer.) Super-8 film costs approximately one dollar per minute plus laboratory costs. Careful shopping for both raw film and lab fees might keep the total cost to one dollar per minute. For a final 15-minute film, you will, according to our rule of thumb, shoot sixty minutes of film (a sixty-dollar film cost). Each copy will cost, for film alone, fifteen dollars.

The cost of videotape for the same program is considerably less. The sixty minutes of original raw footage will cost twenty-five dollars. The final edit will be on a twenty-five-dollar tape also (total cost of fifty dollars). However, once the edit is made, the raw footage can be erased for future programs or for dubs of the edited program. None of the cost of videotape is forever committed to one program.

Third, copies can be made by the organization or person making the program. Editing requires mildly sophisticated equipment, but dubbing (making copies) can be done with any two videotape recorders. The recorders do not have to be alike; they do not even have to be of the same format. In other words, you can make copies of tape from ¾" format machine to the Betamax type of ½" format or to the older, open reel ½" format. Any size or kind of video signal can be dubbed to any other size or format and, of course, to the same size and format. If you can get any two videotape recorders, you can begin to make copies of tapes. But for copies of film you must send your edited original to a laboratory.

EDITING AND REPRODUCTION TECHNIQUES

I have mentioned that editing can be done by reorganizing the original material as you dub it from the original tape to a second tape (called second generation; see below). Let's look first at some of the simple and then at some of the more complex ways of editing.

Videotape recorders without any provision for editing—that is, with no button that says "edit"—cannot make satisfactory edits. The process of putting video signals onto tape requires that the recorder lay a control track on the tape so that the videotape head will trace exactly along the line on which the signal has been recorded. To make good edits, the video track from one machine must be spaced by the control track of the second machine. Therefore, trying to catch those control track spaces by turning the "play" lever of two machines is impossible.

Simple machines that do have "edit" buttons work as follows. To protect videotape material from clumsy operators, the "record" button is locked once the "play" lever is operated. The "edit" button on most simple machines overrides the locking mechanism and will let you change from "play" to "record" modes while the machine is operating. It still takes time for the control track of one machine to coordinate with the video information coming from the other machine.

There are a number of variations on the "edit" button method I have described. However, the only satisfactory method is "electronic editing," using a computerlike console that will interface with videotape recorders designed for this interfacing. These machines are surprisingly inexpensive. Of course, "expensive" and "inexpensive" are relative terms. A church with only one thousand dollars to spend will find proper editing equipment very expensive. However, given the complexity of the equipment and the quality of the work it will do, the cost is comparatively low.

These "electronic editors" overcome the problem of *gliches* because the editing console reads to the control track of both machines and controls the machines together. For more information about the specific techniques of editing, I refer you to Appendix 2 at the end of this book.

In regard to the quality of reproduction, it is a truism that the better the quality of the machines used, the better the reproductions produced. People are accustomed to high quality at the first stage of production; that is, the networks use the best equipment and the most qualified personnel to do a professional job in production. However, by the time the signal reaches our television set, many of us experience less than optimum reception. It is permissible, therefore, when making duplicates for use in church or home, to have reproductions that are of less than broadcast quality. A large loss of quality can be sustained without having the audience aware of the loss. Nevertheless, sloppy production at the beginning will be detected immediately and will identify the producer as an amateur.

Two terms are significant in the making of duplicates and edits: "generations" and "noise." First, "noise" means any part of the signal—audio or video—that is unwanted but inescapable. To get a feeling for what noise is, turn on any piece of electronic equipment, especially audio equipment, where you can hear literal noise. No matter how high the quality of your equipment is, you will hear some sound when there is no signal given. Turn on your stereo and, without putting a record on, listen to the speakers or headset. You will hear some sound—hum, static pops, buzz, etc. The better the quality of audio equipment, the less sound (noise) there will be. This is what is meant by the signal-to-noise ratio of your equipment. A similar range of unwanted electronic signals occur in the video portion of the signal. The original tape has some noise—the better the equipment, the less the noise on the tape. When the original tape is copied over to a second tape, the noise goes with it, and new noise is added by the second recording. And so it continues from generation to generation of tape reproduction.

This does not mean that the more copies you make of a tape, the more the noise will accumulate. Noise is added not by numbers of copies but by numbers of generations. The original tape is called the first generation. If the tape needs no editing—a lecture or speech, for instance, that you are going to reproduce in its entirety—then all of the dubs can be second generation. This means that you will make all of the copies directly from the original.

An edited tape is, *ipso facto,* second generation; that is, the original material is dubbed onto a second tape in the order you want for the final edited version. This makes the edited tape a second generation tape. All of the copies of this tape can be third generation. With the equipment available and in the range of most church organization budgets, there would be little or no loss of quality or increase of noise through the third generation. Making copies of copies beyond the third or fourth generation might reduce quality. The best practice is to make all your copies from the earliest finished generation of tape available.

You might ask if *switching, fading,* and *special effects* can be added in the editing process. The answer is, "Yes, but . . . !" But you will need to use a *time base corrector* (TBC). Even the best videotape recorder is somewhat unstable. Time requirements for video signals are measured in nanoseconds (billionths of a second). Videotape recorders are not stable to within one-billionth of a second. Thus, to use equipment like the switcher fader which requires this kind of time accuracy, you will have to correct the errors inherent in the videotape. The TBC is a very expensive machine and, for that reason, will not soon be a significant part of studio equipment for church and denominational use. Most television stations have time base correctors and can, therefore, play your tapes on their equipment and bring them up to broadcast standards.

There are electronic apparatuses that can correct for noise and other losses of quality. They, too, represent an investment that may not be worth the cost in terms of the final results. You will not experience serious loss of quality if you edit and dub with the equipment I have mentioned as available at a relatively low price. You will not be likely to use special effects in the editing process—these will have to be preplanned and included in the original taping. If any of your tapes are later to be broadcast, the station will provide the time base correction and processing amplification needed to bring the tape up to broadcast quality, provided you have made a high-quality tape for the original.

INCLUSION OF INPUT FROM OTHER MEDIA

While there is good reason to use other media even when television is available, there are also times when you might want to include slides, film, filmstrips, graphics, etc., in a television presentation. Visuals will enhance most presentations. In order to use other media on television, we should be aware of some techniques and some cautions.

A colleague asked why video projection will not soon replace film for theatrical presentations. His impression was that a picture projected onto a screen by one technique must be similar to and therefore interchangeable with the same kind of image projected by another method. This interchange may become possible as the technology changes, but the kind of video now used in broadcasting and for our nonbroadcast applications will never lend itself to theatrical use in the same way film is now projected. Video is suited for the small screen, not only because that is what we are used to, but also because it uses 525 lines of light to produce the picture. No matter how large we project the image, it is still made up of 525 lines. Inclusion of some other media on videotape requires an awareness of some of the significant differences among the various media.

Graphics includes all kinds of artwork, lettering, or illustrations applied to a flat board. In the more sophisticated studio graphics can be *keyed;* that is, lettering can be made to stand out in front of the picture as in the case of the names of participants on the program, or a picture can be made the background and the participants made to appear to be standing in front of it (see *chroma key*). Graphics can be as simple as a graph drawn on newsprint or as complex as an artist's painting.

One key to using graphics well is an understanding of the aspect ratio mentioned earlier. If you are producing graphics for television, you can make sure that they are made to the 3:4 aspect ratio of the TV picture—the picture should be three units high and four units wide. It is important also to keep the graphic material well within very wide margins on the paper or card so that the camera operator will not have difficulty keeping the edge of the card out of the picture. Because individual television sets have differing ways of scanning the picture, you will want to keep the graphics well in from the edges in the camera. This way, none of the graphic information will be lost because of differences in what each television set can reproduce at its edges. A good rule is to keep your graphics in the inner three-quarters of the screen, leaving one quarter of the screen for margin.

There are many ways to produce graphics. One, of course, is to hire an artist to produce them for you. Or you can make them yourself, using the simple transfer methods for lettering, etc., available at most stationery stores.

Slides can be used to enhance video programming just as they are used to enhance a live presentation. Slides can be incorporated into your video presentation in a variety of ways.

The first, and least complex, method is off-the-wall projection. For this method the television camera and the slide projector are aimed at the same spot on a white wall, board, or screen. Because the projector and camera can never be in the same spot (two objects cannot occupy the same space) you will always have a problem with the keystone effect, which occurs whenever you project a picture at an angle other than straight onto the screen. If the projector tilts upward, the top of the picture will be wider than the top of the screen. If the projector projects at an angle from the side, the side farthest from the projector will be larger than the picture portion closer to the projector. One way to compensate for the keystone effect is to keep camera and projector as close as possible; that is, keep the projector and camera at the same height and as nearly as possible at the same angle to the screen. The problem of compensating for keystoning applies to film and all other projections.

The second, and somewhat more complex, method of using slides is with rear-screen projection. Materials for rear screen are available from a number of suppliers at a reasonable price. Attempts to make a

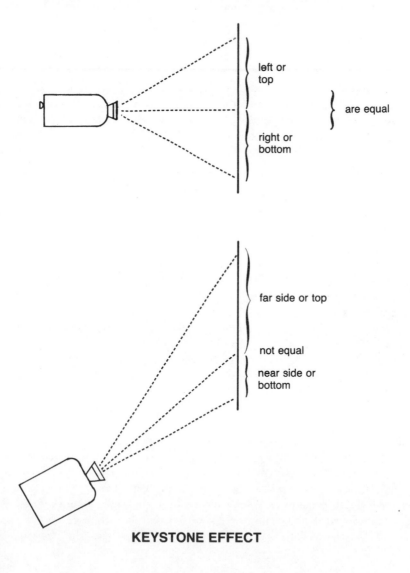

KEYSTONE EFFECT

rear screen from household materials are not worth the effort when you compare effectiveness and cost of the homemade screen with the effectiveness and cost of commercially prepared materials. For rear-screen projection the projector is on one side of the screen and the camera on the other. This will eliminate keystoning—if the projector is at right angles to the screen. This method also allows for a person to be in the picture with the projected image. (Lighting becomes a problem, but it can be done.) In order for the picture to be correct for the camera, it will have to be put into the projector backward. In other words, when viewed from the same side as the projector, the picture will appear backward, with words and signs backward.

You can compensate for the reversal of image through the rear screen with one of two methods. Slides are the most versatile since they can be used with either of the two methods. Slides can be reversed in the projector. If the slide mounts indicate, "This side toward the screen," that side should instead be placed away from the screen. When you put your slides in the wrong way, they will appear right on the other side of the rear screen. Filmstrips and movies cannot be reversed as slides can. The image will have to be reversed with a mirror. The projector projects its image parallel to the screen; the mirror picks up the image and reflects it at a forty-five-degree angle onto the screen. The effect is the lateral reversal of the picture: left is right and right left when viewed from the same side as the projector. Right becomes right again when viewed from the side the camera sees (see illustrations.) The exact angle can be determined through experimentation. You can buy a commercially manufactured instrument called a multiplexer that will take care of the details of rear-screen slide and moving picture film projection. It is a very handy instrument and relatively inexpensive. Yet, compared with the simple rear screen with your own mirror, it is very expensive. Some multiplex systems require the dedication of a camera to the instrument in such a way that the camera cannot be used for other functions. Not all require this investment, however.

Transferring **motion-picture film** to videotape offers some special problems. We could easily get bogged down in some technical jargon and concepts in dealing with the differences between film and videotape. I will limit the discussion to items that are very pertinent to the things you might encounter. Motion-picture film is a whole picture projected onto a surface and changed eighteen or twenty-four times each second. In the jargon of media, a "frame" of motion-picture film consists of

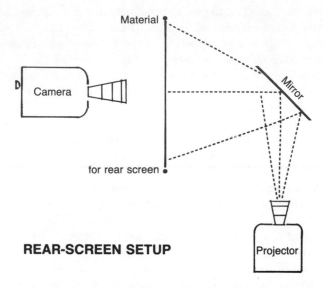

REAR-SCREEN SETUP

a complete picture, but a "frame" of TV picture consists of a dot of light scanning 525 lines thirty times per second. Thus, TV has a rate of thirty frames per second (30 fps). For good transfer of film to video, these frame rates have to be adapted to each other. Projectors for film have been produced that do make this adjustment. Film can be transferred to video without the use of the adapting projector, but you will usually get a dark band that will roll across the face of the picture all the time it is being recorded. A clever tinker can make the adjustment to existing 16-mm projectors to compensate for the differences in fps. I'm not a clever tinker; so I cannot begin to tell you how it is done. Film can be shot by the off-the-wall or the rear-screen process (see the discussion above).

There are some other considerations in the use of film and slides we need to understand to avoid disappointment. First, color film uses a concept of color mixing completely different from that of TV. Video color is additive, while film color is subtractive. If you want to understand this fully I recommend the section on color in Herbert Zettl's book, *Sight, Sound, Motion* (see Appendix 2). I will simply say that this difference will show up if you switch from live colors to film projections. What appears to be just the right color in a slide, and just the right color adjustment of video camera for your live set, may be disappointing when the two are mixed. If you seek color perfection, you will have to invest in quality equipment that can adjust to all these variables. On the other hand, most of us are concerned with conveying information rather than perfection of color. Slides and film will give adequate color information without serious problems.

Second, contrast ratios—the difference between the whitest white and the blackest black—are different for film and TV. Film has a far greater ratio than TV and thus can render shades of difference that video cannot reproduce. This is why you tend to lose detail in night scenes when film is used on TV. When you choose slides or film for television, you will want to make sure that the detail you want is clearly distinguishable on the video screen.

What I have said about slides and film will apply in most cases to any other projected image—overhead projector, opaque projector, etc.

Sound is a medium that we tend to take for granted when we talk about video. We are aware of the need to record the voice of the participant in the program. That in itself presents both problems and opportunities. We are often disappointed in the recordings we make—both audio and video recordings—because the sound is hollow and echoing. You can never really duplicate the quality of studio recordings because those working in studios have engineered their equipment to match the requirements of carefully engineered space. But you can do something to minimize the problems. First, use a room that is acoustically deadened. If a handclap dies off immediately without echo and reverberation, the room is as good as it can be for your purposes. If there is an echo, the room can be furnished with rugs, drapes, and cloth furniture to minimize the echo.

If you use more than one microphone, the speaker's voice may be picked up first on the closer mike then on the other person's mike. The delay caused by the distance between microphones will be recorded as echo. Putting the two microphones out of phase with each other will help eliminate this problem. An electronics hobbyist or ham radio operator— or an electronics engineer—will be able to show you how to change the phase of your microphones.

Good sound from multiple sources requires a sound mixer. You should not simply connect microphones in parallel to a single input, and you cannot parallel high-level sources—phono, tape recorder, cassette player, etc.—with microphones, nor can you plug them into the mike input of your videotape recorder. Sound mixers, like all other electronic equipment, come in a variety of forms and qualities. An acceptable mike mixer can be purchased for as little as twenty dollars. Quality mixers can cost several thousand dollars. The range is almost infinite between these extremes.

You can mix other sound sources—music, other voices (prerecorder), etc.—in your videotape presentation in two ways. First, the music, etc., can be included and mixed at the time of the original taping. This requires careful timing and preparation on the part of the person behind the scene. Second, the music can be added later. Most modern videotape or video cassette recorders are equipped with two sound channels. (Television sets are not now—and so far as I know, will not be in the immediate future—equipped with stereo sound systems.) Therefore, music and other sounds can be added on the second track. This eliminates the possibility of damaging the original track with the additional sound. You will discover variations on these processes by experimenting and by sharing the experiences of others.

Somewhat beyond the scope of the church's use of TV as a teaching instrument is the addition of a video camera to a microscope or a telescope. The connections for both are available from suppliers of video equipment.

Marshall McLuhan suggests that the context of any medium is itself a medium. Television is a picture with sound. Any time you want to show pictures and/or add sound, you can do it with television. You are limited only by your own imagination.

For many reasons a church group might want to tape programs from **broadcast television**—called "off-air taping." A number of contemporary TV programs, secular as well as religious, offer opportunity for discussion. Many programs have become issue oriented and deal with the same issues the church is dealing with. For example, programs like *Mork and Mindy* deal with human communication, violence, compassion, regard for the aging, etc. Others, like *The Paper Chase,* raise questions of values and morals. Some programs offer value orientations with which the church might take issue, for instance, *Love Boat* and most of the "game shows." Since programs are usually on only once (except for summer reruns), it may be difficult for a whole group to see the same program in order to discuss it. Neither movies nor books present this problem. A movie is shown a number of times during its local appearance, and books are available for purchase, sharing, or library borrowing. The only way to guarantee an opportunity for all participants in a discussion to see a specific television program is to tape the program and show it to the group.

But is television worth discussion? Our space is too limited to compare one broadcast season with another in terms of the social contribution of each— the current year is usually considered the worst. Neither is it our purpose to debate the question of popular culture vs. high culture. Let me simply suggest that the hundreds of hours spent with television make television our single most important source of information, entertainment, and myth building.

Taping off-air is not technically difficult. It requires no equipment other than that already within the reach of most churches. Betamax and Video Home Systems have been designed and marketed for the primary purpose of taping programs off-air. It is estimated at the time of this writing that there are three-quarters of a million home videotape recorders and that by 1985 there will be ten million of them. The connection for most of the home videotape recorders is simple. The antenna or cable is connected to the recorder; an output from the recorder connects to the antenna terminal of the TV set. In most cases it is possible to tape one program while you are viewing another. Many of the U-format ¾" recorders are equipped in similar fashion.

Some of the older recorders, especially the ½" open-reel recorders, require a monitor type of TV set in order to tape off-air. The monitor is a specially equipped television set with connectors to the tape recorder for video and audio output and from the recorder back to the TV set. The monitor tends to be heavier and more expensive than an ordinary TV set and for that reason is not as suited to off-air taping as the newer formats. However, if this is the system that is available to you, most high school groups will have a number of students who are familiar with these connections and can handle the process for you.

The legal questions involved are more complex than the technology. When print was the major form of creative production, the copyright law seemed simple and adequate. Sound recordings were not covered by the copyright law until the 1970s. The most recent and most complex copyright law (1976) left ambiguous the matter of television reproduction rights.

While the law is not clear on the specifics of off-air taping, some aspects of the law are clear. It is illegal to sell a copy of a program you have taped. It is improper to make a dub of your copy even to give away. This prohibition is being challenged by hobbyists who collect tapes of programs and share them with other collectors. But if a program is destined to be sold or rented to users in the home or organizational market, it would be improper to make an off-air copy.

Rather than go further with the dos and don'ts of the matter—since some of the dos and don'ts are still in the courts for decision—let me try to derive some guiding principles. It appears clear that the intent of the copyright law is to protect the financial interest of the producer and performer. Whatever might cause damage to that interest would be prohibited by the copyright law. Perhaps you could ask yourself the question, "If everyone with the technological capability I have were to do as I am doing, would there be financial harm to the owner of the copyright?" It would certainly be contrary to the church's value orientation to suggest that because we are small, poor, and in a remote location, no one will ever find out about our tapings.

One other way to help make the judgments required in this complex legal question, to be sure you are violating neither the spirit nor the letter of the law, would be to seek guidance from the educators in your local community They, like the churches, have the need for "fair use" of copyrighted materials. They have legal advice from a variety of sources. You would probably not get into serious trouble if you followed their example.

5

How Does It Work?

In our family we have a set of hand signals that indicate, "You're telling me more than I really want to know!" This may be the way you approach this chapter on the technical operation of television equipment. If you already have a basic knowledge of the workings of a television set or the video cassette recorder, then you may choose to move directly to the next chapter. Our attempt here will be to describe the basic operations involved in video equipment so that some of the mystery will disappear. You should be armed with some information before you begin to negotiate with salespersons. You will also find that technical questions arise in the routine daily setup and operation of your equipment.

THE RECORDING TAPE

Since the audio cassette and 16-mm projector are already familiar to you, we'll use those as tools to help in the understanding of the VCR (video cassette recorder). If you open the front flap of a video cassette by releasing the safety catch, you'll see some plastic tape not unlike that in an audio cassette. The difference is that it is wider and of very high quality. Since pictures, as well as sound, have to be stored on this tape, there's a lot more electrical information to be packed onto a given space on the tape. Recording tape has a coating on a plastic backing. This coating is a metallic oxide that can be magnetized and demagnetized easily. As the tape passes across the recording head of the audio cassette recorder, a tiny magnetic field is impressed on the coating of the tape. These magnetized areas vary in strength and density according to the voice or music that was fed into the recorder. When the tape is played back, the head "reads" these tiny magnetized areas and amplifies them many hundreds of times to give you music or speech.

The typical high quality audio cassette recorder will faithfully reproduce sound frequencies up to about 15,000 hertz or cycles per second. Since the tape is passing the recorder's heads at 1⅞ inches per second, then in any given two-inch piece of tape there could be as many as 15,000 magnetic "changes." The range of human hearing is generally limited to high frequencies at or below this point; so this kind of frequency range or response is quite acceptable.

The recording of video information presents a vastly more difficult problem. Instead of packing fifteen thousand bits of information on the tape every second, it is necessary to pack several million! Neither the recording head nor the playback head can sort this amount of information from a tape that is traveling through the recorder at speeds comparable to those found in an audio recorder. Even professional video recorders only travel at fifteen or thirty inches per second. One solution would be to build a recorder that speeds the tape past the head at close to forty feet per second. At this speed, a thirty-minute audio cassette would last only seven seconds per side!

The solution to this problem came by causing the heads to move at high speed across the face of the tape as the tape moved at a more acceptable speed through the recorder. This is the way in which the currently available machines solve this problem of squeezing a great deal of information on recording tape. This is done in two ways. Broadcast equipment has generally been "quad" or vertical scan. As the tape moves horizontally through the machine, the heads rotate vertically and lay "stripes" of video information on the two-inch wide tape. Four heads are used so that as one head reaches one edge of the tape, the next head is beginning a trace at the other edge of the tape. Since the magnetic lines are very, very narrow, the total length of the recording path on a foot of tape is several hundred feet.

The common industrial and home VCRs use what is called "helical scan." Two heads rotate at high speed horizontally while the tape moves across the head drum at a slight angle. The result is, again, many narrow lines of picture information impressed on a relatively short piece of tape. Many commercial and broadcast users now use one-inch wide tape that is scanned in this helical fashion. The more common industrial and home machines use tape that is either one-half inch or three-quarters of an inch wide.

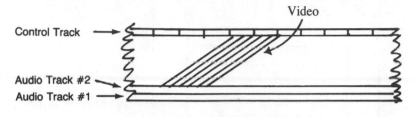

TYPICAL ¾″ VIDEOTAPE

The sound information does not require this kind of treatment to be recorded; so it is added as a linear track on one edge of the tape. You'll notice on the diagram that there is also a *control track*. Here's where your understanding of the movie film and projector will be helpful to our discussion. Movie film has sprocket holes along one edge which are used by the projector to pull the film through the gate one frame at a time and to position the film precisely in front of the lamp. In the instant that the film is stationary, while the advancing pawls are heading for the next set of sprocket holes, the rotating shutter allows light from the lamp to shine through the frame onto the screen. This happens twenty-four times per second on a sound film.

Since the heads as well as the tape are moving in the video recorder, some kind of electronic "sprocket holes" are needed to keep the internal circuitry informed of the position of the lines of picture information on the tape. These control track pulses keep the head motion and tape motion in synchronization so that the recording/play-back head always starts diagonally across the face of the tape at the right time.

THE TELEVISION PICTURE

You have probably noticed that, as you turn your TV set off, the picture will die out as a bright spot in the middle of the screen. This dot, flying across the face of the picture tube at a high rate of speed, is what traces the picture. The dot is really a beam of electrons generated by a gun or guns in the neck of the tube, causing a phosphor coating on the tube to glow. The brightness of the picture at any given instant is relative to the strength of the electron beam.

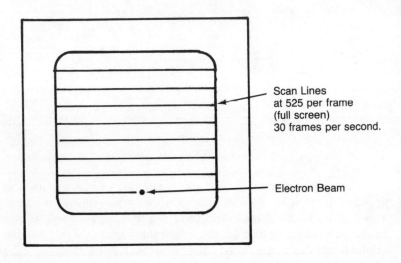

Scan Lines
at 525 per frame
(full screen)
30 frames per second.

Electron Beam

In the U.S. system, there are 525 lines traced across the face of the screen to make up a complete frame. Thirty frames are traced per second. That spot is really moving! Because of the natural retention of images by the eye, we are not aware of the changes that occur as the flying spot flashes back to the top of the screen to begin tracing a new frame. In fact, it's even more complex than that. Each frame is made up of two *fields* of 262½ lines. The first field traces lines 1, 3, 5, 7, etc., and the second fills in 2, 4, 6, etc. It will help you to understand the operation of your VTR when you know that each of the diagonal magnetic stripes or tracks on the videotape contains the information for one of these fields. Two tracks contain a complete frame, and so sixty diagonal magnetic tracks provide one second's worth of television picture. You can understand the need for sophisticated control circuits when you realize how closely packed these lines are and how easily plastic tape can stretch or warp slightly.

COLOR

What we have outlined above is a basic description of the rudiments of both monochrome and color television. Color demands additional complex electronics because the receiver must be given information about color as well as brightness as the spot(s) fly across the screen. Most color television tubes have three electron "guns." Each one of these is set to illuminate the tiny red, blue, or green phosphorescent dots clustered on the face of the screen. (Some manufacturers use extremely narrow stripes, and some use only one electron beam with highly complex aiming and switching circuits.) As you read about VTRs, you'll come across two words that describe the picture information in color television. These are *chrominance,* or color information, and *luminance,* or brightness information. Television cameras, VTRs, and other television control equipment have very accurate crystal "clocks" built in which keep these many signals in the proper relationship to each other. One of the primary differences between expensive broadcast equipment and low-cost home equipment is the tolerances allowed in the various parts of the television signal. The picture produced by an inexpensive camera and VTR, while quite satisfactory for general home or church purposes, will not meet the stringent requirements of the Federal Communications Commission for broadcast. In addition to chrominance and luminance signals, other synchronizing and color control pulses are also present.

SOUND

One of the appeals of using the videotape recorder is that there is instant sound and picture. The sound is always "in sync" with the picture, and some of the common formats allow two completely separate tracks of sound to be recorded at the same time as the picture or even before or later. This provision opens the door to bilingual narration, stereo sound, teacher instruction on one track with pupil instruction on the other, editing information along with sound track, etc. Two-track sound is a very handy feature of the *U* or three-quarter-inch tape format. VTRs generally provide for sound input from radios, tape recorders, and phonographs as well as microphones.

Refer back to the earlier diagram of a section of a typical videotape. You will note that the sound track(s) is recorded along one edge of the tape opposite from the control or "invisible sprocket-hole" track. The sound recording and playback heads are several inches from the rotating picture recording heads. While this distance is fixed and can't get out of synchronization the way a movie projector can, this does present problems for precise editing without specialized equipment. As you have watched news broadcasts with remote field shots, have you ever noticed that there are generally several seconds of picture before the sound is added?

MODULATION

This is another word that you will often see in the instruction books that come with your VTR. We'll take a bit of space to describe how the picture and sound information get to the television receiver. In a later section of this chapter we will be outlining the differences between receivers, receiver/monitors, and monitors.

The weak magnetic pulses that are induced in the rotating video heads, as they pass over the tape, are amplified to a level that would be comparable to that produced by a weak flashlight battery. This signal, while it contains the chrominance and luminance information, is vastly different from that which is received by your television set's antenna. In order to broadcast a television signal, this picture and sound information is mixed with a very high frequency signal—up in the range of the FM broadcast band and far beyond. Each station, of course, has its own assigned frequency. This process is called *modulation,* and what happens in the TV receiver is called *demodulation.* Do you get the picture? Picture and sound signals are mixed with high frequency (VHF and UHF) signals and are then broadcast. These mixed signals are received by the TV set, sorted out by channel, and the picture and sound signals are sorted out and separated once again. The UHF or VHF carrier is then electronically discarded.

What does this have to do with videotape recording? All of the home model VTRs have what is called a modulator built in. This is a small, very low power transmitter which does just what we have been describing. The picture and sound signals from the tape are mixed with a VHF signal (generally channel 3 or 4) so that the resulting signal can be connected to the VHF antenna terminals of an ordinary set and be received by it on the chosen channel.

The more professional machines may not have the built-in modulating capability, and so playback must be through specially designed TV sets which will be described later. On these machines, picture and sound signals are handled separately with different kinds of cables. There is some loss in the quality of the picture each time the signal is mixed and unmixed. Therefore, systems requiring optimum quality will not use a modulator. The home-format machines do, however, have separate video and sound inputs and outputs so that they can be used with a camera or a monitor. Two or more home format machines can also be connected together for tape duplicating, using these input and output jacks and plugs.

CAMERAS

Television cameras range in price from a few hundred dollars for a simple, home-television, black-and-white model to over one hundred thousand dollars for a top-of-the-line broadcast color camera. At the heart of all of these cameras is a tube which converts light to electrical impulses. The wide variations in price are a function of quality, sensitivity, accuracy, and additional features. Broadcast cameras generally have three pick-up tubes, one for each of the primary colors. Some industrial cameras use two tubes—one to translate luminance information and the other to provide chrominance information. Many of the newer low-cost color cameras are single-tube devices. The signal produced by this camera is similar to those in VTRs and TV receivers. Sixty fields and thirty frames are scanned every second. Some cameras even have small modulators built in so that they can be used directly with a TV receiver tuned to the appropriate channel.

TAPE FORMATS

There are four common videotape formats at the present time. Because of the cost of the first two types of equipment, most churches will not be able to consider their use, but we'll describe them briefly.

Quad. This has been the common broadcast-quality format for many years. The tape is two inches wide and is scanned by four video heads moving perpendicular to the length of the tape. Recorders may cost well over one hundred thousand dollars each with their support equipment.

One-inch. Many broadcast and industrial users are moving to a newly standardized one-inch tape format. The tape is scanned diagonally across the face of the tape (helical scan), just like the less expensive machines, but the quality and precision are very high and, therefore, so is the price.

"U" or three-quarter-inch cassette. This format was for many years the common educational and industrial format. The cassette protected the delicate tape and made it easy to distribute programs. Up to an hour could be recorded on the standard cassette. These features, combined with reasonable costs (in the range of $1,500 to $6,000) made this the common equipment of the past few years.

One-half-inch Beta and VHS. These are the two formats which have created the revolution in home video recording. The cartridges used by these two types of machines are not compatible, but the tape inside the cassette is the same. Each group of manufacturers has decided on a unique way of threading the tape inside the VTR as well; however, tapes recorded on one Beta-type machine will be playable on another. The same holds true of the VHS format. There are different recording speeds available with both types of machines, however, and this could limit interchangeability. Most home-style VTRs now have a "long-play" speed which, at the sacrifice of some quality, gives twice the recording time on a tape. Tapes must, of course, be played at the same speed at which they were recorded.

One of the earliest nonbroadcast tape formats put to good use by industry, education, and churches was the half-inch open reel. Some manufacturers still make this type of equipment, and a good many of these machines are still in use. Some of the better open-reel recorders were good quality color machines with full editing capabilities. Most manufacturers have dropped this equipment from their catalogs, but a church wishing to develop carefully edited programs might find a good value in used equipment of this type.

You might come across some other formats which are no longer very common. Several companies have manufactured one-inch machines, but there were problems and struggles with standardization. There have also been some attempts made to use one-quarter-inch-wide tape in both open reel and cassette. Publicity is beginning to appear in trade journals about half-inch cassette machines which will record up to eight hours on a cassette. The tape will be flipped over to use the other side of the tape in a manner similar to audio cassettes. These tapes will not be compatible with the Beta and VHS machines.

EDITING AND SPLICING

If you have worked at all with open-reel audio tape recorders, you know that very elaborate editing can be accomplished by cutting and splicing pieces of tape together. Words can be literally cut out by removing an inch or so of tape. Careful editors can even remove a room noise or an unwanted *s* on the end of a word. Four problems arise when one tries to handle videotape in this manner. (1) The information is packed onto the tape with such density that a cut would affect several frames. (2) A cut will disturb the control track and cause the machine to lose synchronization for an instant, thus causing the picture to roll.

(3) Since the recording is diagonally across the tape, a vertical cut will interrupt many picture fields and frames and will be very noticeable during playback.(4) Video heads are moving at a high rate of speed and are pressed hard against the tape. Any ridges or foreign material on the tape can damage these delicate heads.

In the early years of videotaping, systems were devised for making the record lines visible so that technicians could actually try to cut between the lines. It was always a very chancy task. The above comments should serve as a warning to you to *try not to cut and splice videotape physically*. Tape that is damaged should probably be discarded unless you have some considerable skill in making repairs. Splicing and editing of program segments is done electronically by erasing old material and replacing it instantly with new program.

CABLES AND CONNECTORS

Another way in which videotape equipment is different from that used just for audio work is in the kinds of cables and connectors used. Your home television antenna or cable system might use a round coaxial cable with a single copper conductor surrounded by foam or plastic, covered with a copper braided shield and a heavy plastic outer coating. This is type "59" coaxial cable, and it is the common "pipe" for video signals. The common connectors used are either UHF or BNC. The UHF connectors are screw type, while the BNC are a quick release type, using a collar which releases and connects with a quarter turn. Newer industrial equipment seems to be standardizing with the BNC-type connectors. A note is in order here. The cable used is not unlike the 50-ohm cable used for CB radio antennas, but the impedance is different. Be sure you always use 75-ohm cable with your video equipment. By the way, these cables will break internally with twisting, kinking, and coiling. Handle them *very carefully*. Cables are always suspect as the first culprit when your system will not work. Some home-model machines use RCA-type connectors for video as well as audio connections.

Audio cables are more routine but demand the same type of careful handling. All of these cables are shielded to prevent interference from outside electrical sources, such as house power lines, electric motors, etc. Check to see whether the microphone you are using is called "low impedance" or "high impedance." High-impedance microphone wires must be kept reasonably short because of the deterioration of the signal in these lines. If your installation calls for long audio cables, consult with a knowledgeable person regarding the proper types of cables, microphones, and transformers to use. Lengths of 15 feet or less will not cause you any problems.

If your VTR has a built-in tuner for receiving and recording television broadcasts, then you will find connectors on the rear of the machine for UHF and VHF antennas. A type *F* connector is generally used for cable-type antenna connections.

MONITORS, MONITOR/RECEIVERS, RECEIVERS

It was mentioned above that the kind of signal or electrical information that comes from a videotape is unusable at the antenna of an ordinary TV set. This picture information must be mixed with the sound and then onto a carrier or broadcast signal tuned to a common television channel—generally channel 3 or channel 4.

Special equipment is available to translate this video signal into a usable picture without going through the modulating and demodulating process. The monitor/receiver is a TV set with connectors and switches which allow the user to disconnect the broadcast signal from the later stages of the TV set's circuitry and replace it with the video information from a camera, VTR, special effects generator, color bar generator, or other pieces of specialized equipment. These monitor/receivers, while more expensive than an ordinary TV set, will provide higher quality pictures and will most often allow recording programs "off the air" onto VTRs which do not have built-in tuners. In this regard, one such monitor/receiver can be a good investment if you are purchasing industrial half-inch or three-quarter-inch equipment which might not have built-in tuners and modulators. The video monitor is a picture tube and the electronic circuits needed to control it with no provision for receiving broadcast information. It may or may not have sound built in. This is the type of equipment used with security cameras or in the television studio and control room. A small black-and-white monitor will cost as little as $250, while an extremely accurate color monitor for professional use in critical applications might run in the range of $3,000 to $5,000.

6

How to Get Started

Once you have decided that videotaping capability would be an asset to your church's program, your natural inclination might be to begin to study catalogs and to contact sales representatives. There are several prior questions which must be answered. If you and the appropriate committee have worked through some of your unique plans and problems, you will be better able to sort out the data that is of primary interest to you from sales presentations and technical specification sheets.

QUESTIONS YOU NEED TO ASK

There is another most important reason for careful planning. The video industry is a rapidly changing one. Equipment lines are superseded by new models every few months. Hardware that was the state of the art two years ago might now be dropped from catalogs or even be obsolete as a format. There is no way for the church with a modest budget to stay up-to-date by always owning the very latest equipment. Careful planning will help you put together a system which will be compatible and useful for your own purposes, even though the consumer market has moved far ahead. Your plans should include a realistic anticipation of the useful life of VTRs (videotape recorders), VCRs (video cassette recorders), and other associated pieces with some plan and budget for maintenance and replacement.

How Will This Equipment Be Used?

Take time to explore all the possible (but realistic) ways in which your new recording capability might serve you. (The "realistic" qualification is there to remind you that we are discussing nonbroadcast video. Unless you can make a sizeable investment in hardware, space, and personnel, your programs will not be suitable for broadcast.) A thorough understanding of anticipated uses, as well as your limitations, will help you and salespersons design a system which will develop consistently as your needs change.

The very simplest system will lend itself nicely to individual and "in-house" use. A VCR with a built-in tuner can be used to store broadcast material for viewing in whole or in part at a more convenient time. Be advised, however, that broadcast material is protected by copyrights. Use of this program material without permission is generally restricted and often prohibited. A "playback-only" machine will give you access to the ever-expanding libraries of prerecorded material. These tapes are often copies of films and rent for approximately the same cost. Your choice of a tape or a film should be determined by intended use.

A VCR, camera, and television set will open the door to teachers' self-analysis, microteaching (a technique of training and evaluation that concentrates on one teaching skill at a time), worship evaluation, and other uses discussed elsewhere in this book.

Do you hope to share your programs with others? If you plan to move in this direction eventually, then thought should be given to the quality of the finished product and the kind of equipment needed to allow you to edit both sound and picture. A simple black-and-white camera will generally operate satisfactorily in a normally lighted room for such tasks as classroom observation or teacher evaluation. Tapes of this nature will most likely be used once and then erased. Programs designed to be used by others who were not present during the original taping will need to be of much higher quality. Your initial equipment purchases should be made as a compromise between your budget and future needs. Cable television provides an opportunity for many churches to originate and share programs, but a substantial budget is needed to do this properly.

Color or Black-and-White?

The world is in color! It has been reported that there is no evidence that persons learn any more readily from a color than from a black-and-white program. We are, however, so thoroughly accustomed to color in every other setting that a potential purchaser should consider this option seriously. The newer VCRs are, of course, all color compatible. The point at which you will make your major choice will be in the purchase of a camera and, to a lesser extent, a receiver or monitor.

Space, Storage, and Transportation?

A simple system will not create any insurmountable space and handling problems. One-half-inch consumer-type VCRs can be easily handled by one person even up and down stairs. A color television receiver is another matter! Nineteen-inch sets weigh in at a hefty sixty to seventy pounds. This equipment is best handled by using a tall two-shelf audiovisual cart which can be stored easily as a unit. Your choice of a receiver size should be based, at least in part, on the strength of the persons who will be handling it. Consider the question of security as well. This type of equipment is most attractive to thieves.

Personnel and Training?

Your prepurchase discussions should also cover the training of persons in the proper handling and use of equipment. As you accept bids from dealers and discuss your needs, the question of continuing help can be an important nonfinancial item. In addition to help from your dealer in learning to use your equipment to its fullest potential, make arrangements to take advantage of other training possibilities. Don't ignore the instruction manuals! In fact, it's a good idea to file the original copy in a safe place and make a few copies to stay with the hardware. Several manufacturers produce training tapes on all phases of videotape production and operation. Ask your distributor about rental of these materials, or check with the AV department of a nearby school. One of the best informal television training programs is around all the time. Begin to watch broadcast TV from the viewpoint of camera operator, director, or editor. You will not have any sophisticated switching and special effects equipment at your disposal, but you can begin to develop a sense of timing and movement which will serve you in good stead in even simple one-camera productions.

Which Manufacturer's Products?

All of us tend to have favorite brands, and the loyalties we feel are not always based on objective data. You may have stuck with one brand of automobile through thick and thin for a number of logical and illogical reasons. Your choice of brands and formats in video equipment will be based, of course, on the price, features, and performance specifications of a particular manufacturer's products. You should, however, give a good deal of weight to the availability of dealer service and support. If you are providing a regularly scheduled program to a local cable outlet, a replacement unit loaned by your dealer while your unit receives service can be worth more than the dollars saved by buying from a distant dealer with a lower bid. Check to see that local dealers have on-site repair capability for the equipment you plan to purchase. Sophisticated test equipment and procedures are a part of maintaining and repairing VTRs and might be beyond the scope of a shop set up for television service only.

If possible, arrange for demonstrations of different brands of equipment at your church. This will give you some information about portability and the complexity of system set-up. Try the system out in the rooms where you plan to do most of your taping. Ask questions of those who are working with similar equipment for recommendations. Are there features that these persons particularly like or have found to be a nuisance? Would they buy the same piece of equipment now? Does the dealer give good support?

Your choice of tape format might also be largely determined by your plan to participate in a library or sharing arrangement with other users. Some commercial libraries do not provide tapes in every size and type. A denomination might encourage all of its member churches to work with one common tape format.

If you already are using some videotape equipment or you plan to purchase hardware from more than one manufacturer, check to be sure that all pieces can be interconnected and will be compatible.

Your dealer can also keep you abreast of the most recent developments in the field of video so that you are not always buying into obsolescence. There will always be a new model around the corner, but a wait of a few weeks and the expenditure of a few extra dollars might buy you a significant improvement in quality or convenience.

SAMPLE SYSTEMS

Several representative systems will be considered in this chapter with approximate "low" and "high" cost figures. The low-cost figure will generally represent the minimally acceptable equipment to be used with the other suggested hardware. This means that as the quality of the overall system improves, the quality of the individual pieces will also need to be upgraded. The total package may be only as good as its weakest component. Cameras and VTRs are the two most critical pieces of equipment you will be considering.

The simplest system would, of course, be a videotape player (one without any recording capability) and a TV receiver. This combination will, however, not be recommended to churches beginning in the use of video unless used or obsolete equipment can be purchased at a very good price. Video players are available in the industrial grade machines, but their cost, because of extra features useful for sales presentations and editing, is as high or even higher than a full-feature consumer recorder. Owning a player will limit you to using materials produced by others.

A word needs to be said about electrical demand by your system. The VCR, camera, and TV will require only a few hundred watts of power and can be fed by common extension cords. A basic lighting kit, however, will need about 1,800 watts and should operate from a 20-amp fused circuit with no other demand on it at the time of your recording.

Several manufacturers produce sets in either the VHS or Beta format. Consumer models in VHS are generally 2/4 hours at this time. The newer Beta machines will record in the 4-hour format but will automatically play back tapes recorded at the earlier 1- and 2-hour speeds. Tapes vary in length as well. The times mentioned are for the longest tapes and slowest speeds as of this writing. This information will very likely change soon! One manufacturer is now showing an 8-hour machine with a tape which flips over to record on two sides. This will be a third noncompatible format.

Industrial grade machines may or may not have tuners and generally operate at only one recording speed. The higher cost features on this equipment include such items as slow motion, stop action, single frame, higher speed forward and reverse motion, and computer-controlled random search. Some of these machines can also serve as source players for an automated editing system. The Beta industrial machines operate at the one-hour speed, while the VHS industrial machines are two-hour recorders and players. Several companies have a battery-operated recorder which, when coupled with a battery-operated camera, will give you complete freedom for recording in an outdoor setting.

Cost estimates are based on manufacturers' suggested retail prices. Shop carefully, weighing service and dealer support against price. Discounts in the range of 10 percent to 20 percent are not uncommon, and special promotional packages are often available.

System No. 1

The minimum investment will include a consumer model VCR with a built-in tuner to receive UHF and VHF television broadcasts and a black-and-white or color television receiver. If you use a black-and-white receiver for playback or monitoring of programs, this will in no way affect the color of the program on the tape, and it will play back properly in color on a color set. A word of warning is in order here. If you use a black-and-white set, be sure to follow the manufacturer's instructions for adjusting the VCR's tuner, since your black-and-white television set will not be able to indicate a slight tuning variation which might cause loss of proper color.

Consumer model VCR	$1,000-$1,400
Industrial model VCR	$1,000-$2,000
TV receiver (b/w or color)	$125-$450

Both of these types of machines, in either the VHS or Beta format, will record from a black-and-white or color camera. The industrial machine may not be able to record from the air, but it may have features attractive to you if you plan to expand your system to include editing at a later date. The consumer machine will be very adequate for recording broadcasts (be aware of the laws regarding the illegal use of such recorded material), playing prerecorded tapes, and recording both sound and picture from a camera and microphone.

System No. 2

In this system we have added a black-and-white or color camera, a basic lighting kit of three 600-watt quartz lights with reflectors and stands, three inexpensive microphones, cables, and a simple microphone mixer. The more expensive lighting system will include heavier stands and focusable lamps. A good guideline to remember is that a three-light kit (1,800 watts) will light an area 10 feet square to about 140 *foot candles* in a room with normal reflection from the walls and ceiling. This is the minimum recommended illumination for color cameras for the best picture quality. Newer inexpensive cameras will operate with much less light, but there is a noticeable drop in picture quality.

Black-and-white cameras will operate in ranges of 2- to 5-foot candles, but lights will improve picture quality and help control shadows.

VCR (consumer or industrial model)	$1,000-$2,000
Camera (b/w or color)	$300-$1,500
TV receiver (b/w or color)	$125-$450
Three-light kit (1,800 watts)	$150-$400
Three low-cost microphones	$75
Simple sound mixer (a/c or battery)	$50-$120
Tripod and dolly	$175

System No. 3

Some churches have found it useful to have portable equipment to allow freedom to move throughout the building and community without the restriction of having to connect to power lines. In the VHS and Beta machines, the maximum recording time on a fully charged battery is one hour. The power demand of newer equipment is being lowered, however, and so this battery time might be extended in later models. These are industrial machines and may not have tuners or extended play capability.

Each manufacturer supplies a camera or cameras which will mate directly with the recorder and possibly even derive power from it. These cameras generally have a built-in microphone, and all connections to the recorder are made through one multiconnector cable.

Portable VCR	$1,400
Portable camera	$1,400
TV receiver or receiver/monitor	$125-$800
Lighting kit, tripod, dolly	$325-$575
Microphones and mixer	$125-$200

You will find that the built-in microphone is quite inadequate in most situations because of room and background noise. You'll need separate microphones and a mixer. A higher cost receiver/monitor will allow off-the-air recording.

System No. 4

This system is based on a change in format to the *U* or ¾″ tape cassette. The more expensive ¾″ equipment has better electronic specifications than the ½″ hardware, but this difference will not be noticeable to the casual viewer. At the present state of the art, the ¾″ cassette opens the door to the possibility of sophisticated editing of programs and wider distribution to cable and even some local broadcast outlets. The wider tape has greater resistance to stretch and warp and is, therefore, able to maintain a more stable signal with more accurate timing. Some television stations use this type of equipment for commercials and remote news gathering.

¾″ cassette recorder with tuners	$2,200
Camera (b/w or color)	$600-$3,000
Lights, tripod, and dolly	$325-$575
Mixer and microphones	$125-$200
TV receiver or receiver/monitor	$125-$800

The price range on the camera has been expanded to include color cameras which can be interfaced with mixing and switching equipment at a later date.

System No. 5

This system will continue with the ¾″ format but will build upon a portable recorder and camera. Both camera and recorder will be of more professional quality than the comparable portable ½″ equipment, although a high quality camera can certainly be used with Beta and VHS recorders. Currently available U or ¾″ portable cassette machines are limited to the use of the smaller S-size tape cassettes which will run for twenty minutes. (There are 30-minute extended-play tapes available with very thin tape inside. These are much more liable to be chewed up by a machine that is slightly out of alignment.)

These ¾″ portables are very high quality machines. Many feature automatic assemble edits. Each time a new scene is started, the mechanism locks up to the earlier control pulses and automatically switches during the *vertical interval*. Some have two audio tracks and batteries which will run for two hours. Tapes can be placed directly on editors to build longer programs or add remote segments to studio material.

Portable ¾″ recorder	$3,000
Color camera (directly mates to the recorder)	$3,000
Lights, microphones, mixer, tripod, dolly	$500-$1,100

Color receiver, receiver/monitor,
    or monitor $450-$800

System No. 6

This is an improvement over the studio ¾″ system described in System No. 4. The basic change is in the purchase of a master editor which will allow full control of video and two tracks of audio. Such a machine will be able to make recordings of up to an hour in length on *U* format cassettes. Both "assemble" and "insert" edits will be possible. Assemble editing adds one program segment after another as in the splicing of movie film. Insert editing leaves the control track undisturbed but replaces the video or audio or both with new material. Using this feature, slides can be put into a program, for instance, after it is recorded, or one can go back and add close-ups of a demonstration while leaving the sound track undisturbed. Such a machine can also become the heart of a full automatic system described later.

¾″ recorder with full electronic editing $6,300-$6,600
Color camera $3,000-$4,000
Lights, sound equipment, tripod,
    and dolly $500-$1,100
Color monitor or monitor/receiver $600-$800

This type of recorder will very likely not have an output modulator (the small transmitter to broadcast picture and sound to the TV set's antenna through a length of cable). You will need to invest in a good quality monitor or monitor/receiver.

System No. 7

This expensive package will be of interest only to those churches, agencies, or institutions planning to produce high quality programs for distribution to others. This sharing might be through a rental or lending arrangement with other churches or local cable outlets. Be advised that these costs could be the tip of the iceberg, since no provision is made for development of a studio or hardwiring and lighting a sanctuary and the time of the people involved in such an elaborate arrangement. This is the type of equipment that many educational and industrial studios use to develop "in-house" training materials. If your plans include an eventual editing or multicamera small studio capability, make arrangements to visit some industrial video operations for suggestions and realistic cost projections.

Slave and master ¾″ recorders with automatic controller	$9,600-$17,000
Color monitor/receiver or monitor	$600-$1,500
B/w monitor, 9″ with *cross pulse* (see glossary)	$400
Color camera (portable with studio adaptability)	$3,000-$5,000
Portable recorder (either ½″ or ¾″ format)	$1,400-$3,000
Lighting, sound equipment, tripod, dolly	$600-$1,200

The use of a BETA or VHS portable recorder will lower quality a bit because of extra "dubbing" or transferring, but there is some saving, and it will give you access to another format.

System No. 8

This system, like No. 7, will only be of interest to those who wish to establish a reasonable cost production capability to originate materials for distribution either through a library-sharing arrangement or on a regularly scheduled use of local cable television.

Because of the complexity of the color television signal, elaborate equipment is needed to control and mix the outputs from more than one camera. A special effects generator/switcher will allow the operator to choose video from one of several cameras or mix and fade these outputs together. Video from a high quality ¾″ recorder can also be intermixed with video from cameras.

Special effects generator/switcher	$2,500-$8,000
Rack-mount three- or four-screen monitors	$900-$1,800
Rack-mount sound mixer	$250-$500
Distribution amplifiers	$700-$1,500

In addition to the above, there is, of course, the cost of cameras, microphones, lights, tripods, dollies, cables, and intercoms. Operating such a system also requires the time of at least three persons during production.

7

Tricks and Hints

A quick glance through the catalogs and trade journals of the television industry will make you aware of the plethora of available equipment. There is a specialized cart, gizmo, or gadget for every application. Some of these items are good investments, but others can be produced with a few hours' work in the shop of a willing craftsman.

CARTS

Color television receivers large enough to be comfortably viewed by a group of twenty-five or so people, are heavy. You will probably want to build or purchase a tall cart which can be used to move your receiver and VCR around the building. If you will frequently have to negotiate stairs, consider one of the manufactured carts with large rear wheels and straps to anchor equipment on the shelves. The rear wheels need to be as large as possible with rubber tires to be able to negotiate stairs without equipment-shattering bumps. With a well-balanced cart, over one hundred pounds of equipment can be moved easily.

Pick up pictures of these commercially available carts. Many basic designs can be easily duplicated with simple tools using plywood or thin-wall conduit. Thin-wall comes in 10-foot lengths in several diameters. Electricians have bending jigs for this tubing, or they can be purchased at reasonable cost if you plan to build much of your own equipment. Connectors are available for thin-wall tubing at hardware and electrical supply houses. By the use of tubing and threaded steel rod (which comes in lengths up to 6 feet) strong, lightweight carts can be fabricated.

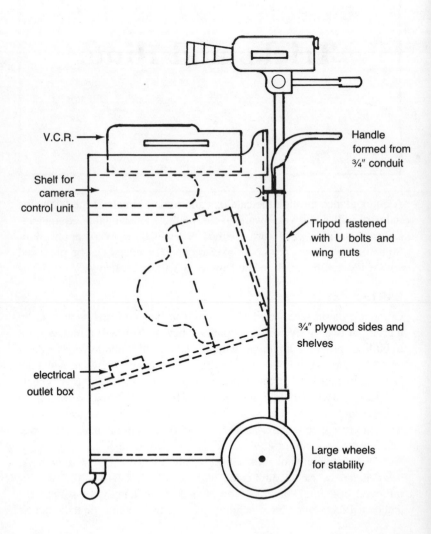

This handy cart can become a mobile production center. The tripod is clamped to the rear support with *U* bolts and wing nuts so that it can be easily removed. The receiver is slanted so that you can view the picture easily, and the VCR's controls are easily accessible. The ½″ axle is a piece of steel rod available at any hardware store. One-half-inch copper pipe clips can be used to fasten the axle to the body of the cart. Front wheels should be steerable casters.

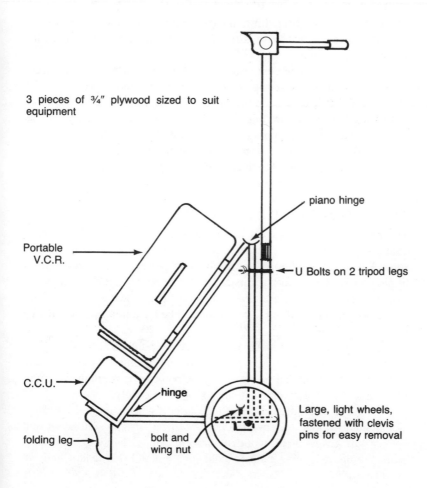

3 pieces of ¾″ plywood sized to suit equipment

piano hinge

Portable V.C.R.

U Bolts on 2 tripod legs

C.C.U.

hinge

Large, light wheels, fastened with clevis pins for easy removal

folding leg

bolt and wing nut

A similar cart for use with your portable equipment will fold to fit into the trunk of a car. Portable VCRs are designed to operate in any position, but do not attempt to operate your consumer machine in any position other than horizontal. Check your instruction manual for these limitations.

The wheels on any of these carts should be as large and light as possible. Large wheels with tires will help you negotiate stairs, thick carpet, rough sidewalks, and bumpy ground.

STORAGE

VCRs all come with a plastic fitted cover. Use it. There's always the danger of liquids or dirt getting into the mechanism while it's in storage. Be sure, however, that there is free air movement around your machine while it is operating.

Keep the shipping containers and the foam inserts for each piece. These are excellent for storage and are particularly good for transporting your equipment. Cement the bottom fitted inserts in place in the bottom of the box for easier handling. Reinforce the corners and edges of the box with glass fiber strapping tape *before* it starts to fall apart.

A good supply of nylon straps in various lengths can be very handy. These can be used to anchor equipment to carts, serve as handles for boxes, and bundle tripods and dollies for transport or storage.

CAMERA TRIPODS AND DOLLIES

The lightweight tripods used in still photography are simply not adequate for your television camera. Be sure the head of your tripod has some kind of "antidump" mechanism to protect your camera from tipping forward accidently. This can dislodge minute specks of material from the rear of the picture tube and cause a permanent speck to appear on the screen. This "dump" protector will be a friction lock or a heavy spring.

If your budget can stand it, consider the purchase of a *fluid head* tripod. These are particularly good with single-camera systems where you will be panning and tilting while the recorder is running. Friction-type tripod heads are very difficult to move smoothly.

Purchase a folding dolly with the largest wheels possible. Professional studio floors are smooth, but you'll be working on carpet and uneven surfaces. A small wooden platform can be clamped to the dolly with *U* bolts and wing nuts to hold the camera control unit and a/c power supply.

LIGHTING

The less expensive lighting kits generally come with lightweight stands of insufficient height. You will very likely be working in settings where you will not be able to mount lights permanently to the ceiling. In order to keep shadows as low in the picture as possible, your lights need to be placed high. Your light stands should be able to extend to at least 8 feet. If your budget does not allow for a better grade of lighting kit, purchase the parts separately and invest in at least two heavy-duty light stands. These heavy-duty stands will also allow you to use photographers' "umbrellas" to give you soft, almost shadow-free lighting. Another option is to invest in a single 1,500-watt professional softlight. They're expensive but very useful.

A canvas athletic equipment bag is a handy way to transport and store tripods and light fixtures. Store the quartz bulbs, wrapped in their foam liners, in a plastic, compartmented parts box. Oil from your fingers will shorten the life of these bulbs. Wrap them in tissue, and use the tissue to insert the bulbs in the reflectors. BE SURE THE LAMP IS UNPLUGGED when you insert bulbs. Quartz lamps heat up instantly, and you can be burned badly in an instant. With proper care, these lamps will last as long as 75 hours, but you should, of course, keep an inventory of spares handy.

Some fixtures in the less expensive kits come with light-duty switches on the lamp cord. These generally prove to be troublesome after repeated use. Have someone familiar with electrical wiring bypass these switches. A handy lamp control box can be made as follows: Cut the female end off a heavy-duty three-wire extension cord. Mount a double grounded outlet and a single outlet with switch in a square metal electrical junction box with metal cover. Wire the switch so that it controls the three outlets. Be sure to use a cable clamp for strain relief where the extension cord enters the box. This will give you a heavy-duty, switchable distribution box for your lights. If you make up two of these, one should have about 100 feet of heavy extension cord so that you will be able to tap into a separate circuit in another room of your building. In this way, extra lights may be added without tripping circuit breakers.

For visual variety, use a *cookie*. This is a mask perforated with random holes or a pattern which is placed in front of a light aimed at the background. In this way, a plain plaster wall can be given an interesting texture.

Twenty-five dollars worth of fabric from the local sewing center can also do wonders for your sets. Keep several pieces of cloth about 4 feet square on hand to cover tables or place over easels. Several widths of 8-foot-long medium blue cloth can be draped on wire or a piece of light tubing and fastened to the wall to give you a controlled background. In this way window light can be controlled, and unwanted sections of the room can be covered. Picture-hanging wire and hooks work nicely as a temporary support. If camera angles are kept low, the top part of your makeshift drape will not show on camera.

SOUND

Our hearing adjusts to background noises in rooms, and we are not aware of them until the recording is played back. Check out your room with a cassette recorder, or make a preliminary test recording with the microphones connected to your VTR. It is very likely that you will not be able to control many of the annoying background sounds in the rooms where you will be working; so you should plan to use unidirectional microphones fairly close to the persons who are speaking on camera. Don't worry about concealing mikes. TV viewers are accustomed to seeing microphones in every setting except dramas. Your greatest problem will be to keep "talent" from absentmindedly rubbing the mike or playing with the cord. Train yourself to hear these sounds before they're on tape.

Electret lavaliere mikes are relatively inexpensive and work quite well. The quality is not always consistent even within the same brand, however; so arrange for a replacement if it has poor quality. You will not have this problem if you invest in better-quality microphones. Remove the batteries from electret mikes after each use. Some have a nasty habit of draining the battery fairly quickly.

Another item to check out before you purchase a VTR is the ALC or automatic level control. Some machines use ALC, while others use a switchable limiter which only compresses the loudest sounds. Some ALC circuits tend to "hunt" when there is no sound near the microphones. Some inexpensive microphones can also compound this problem. This can be checked by operating the recorder in a quiet room and then speaking into the mike at normal voice level. A poor ALC circuit will cause a gradual rise in the level of room background noise with a sudden drop when speech is recorded. This was a particularly annoying problem on some earlier machines without manual volume controls. Check this feature out as a part of your comparison shopping.

If you plan to use several microphones in interview or panel discussion settings, it helps to cable the microphone extension cords together. There are commercially produced "snakes" which connect a junction box for several mikes to a sound mixer through a multiconductor cable. Such a "snake" can be easily made up by someone with some mechanical skill. It should be about 25 feet long. Use broadcast-type connectors in the junction box, and spend the time and few dollars to replace the "miniplugs" commonly found on low-cost microphones with Cannon-type connectors. Be sure to make the proper connections for your mixer's balanced or unbalanced inputs. The mixer instruction sheet will describe the proper procedure. These heavy-duty connectors will save you the grief of noisy audio caused by poor connections.

A very handy plastic spiral wrap for cables is available from electronic supply houses. With this product you can neatly cable and protect wires that will always interconnect the same pieces of equipment. Do not, however, run power lines alongside audio and video lines for any distance. Alternating current hum can be induced in both video and audio lines in this way.

EDITING

Consider the purchase of a machine with electronic editing capability if you plan to develop programs to be shared with other groups or used as a teaching tool. Electronic editing will allow the insertion of slides, close-ups of charts, videotape recorded at another time, titles, pictures, music, etc. This type of equipment is expensive when purchased new, but your needs might well be served by used open-reel ½" equipment with this full electronic editing capability. These machines have been superseded by the higher quality automated ¾" editors, but they were the standard of the industrial/educational market for many years and are capable of excellent picture quality. There are two main drawbacks to the open-reel editors. They are manually operated and therefore more difficult to time accurately, and they have only one audio track.

There are a couple of tricks which will help in the timing of single machine edits. Point your camera at an accurate digital clock while recording the entire tape. Use the "insert" edit function to build your program. The recording of the clock will allow you to leave accurately timed sections for later insertion of new material. If your recorder has two sound tracks, record a time track by counting minutes and seconds into a microphone connected to one of the tracks. Program audio will go on the other. Turn off the "record" switch for this track. Edit points on your tape can now be noted to the second. When you back up the cassette to begin an edit, the time track will serve as a "count up" to the point where you will make the edit. A second recorder can also be cued the same way to provide semiautomatic editing between two machines. It is possible to use this same method with single-track machines by preserving the audio on a stereo sound recorder with the time count on the second channel. Replace the audio on the VTR with a time count, and after editing is complete, rerecord the original sound track from the stereo recorder. Good luck!

Single-camera productions suffer from a lack of visual variety and are often "talking-head" productions. Postproduction editing will allow the insertion of complementary material while leaving the audio and control tracks undisturbed.

If you can borrow a second camera and recorder, there's a way to produce a two-camera program without the complex switching equipment that is usually needed to synchronize two color cameras. The entire program can be handled by one person. Set up one camera for a wide shot of the set, and start the recorder. Move the other camera, and use the zoom lens to feature reaction shots or close-ups of participants and visuals. Edit sections of one tape into the other at appropriate points. Make a copy of the master tape first so that your trial and error will not destroy material you might want to use again.

COLOR ADJUSTMENTS

Several companies make color-adjusting charts for color cameras and monitors, but your receiver or receiver/monitor can be adjusted using a network television broadcast. The color from a popular late evening, nationally broadcast talk show is always superb. Carefully adjust your set on the flesh tone of the host. You'll get plenty of ECU shots with which to work. Mark the contrast, color, and tint controls of your set for future reference, or remove these knobs. Using this standard, adjust your camera's controls for accurate flesh tones. You'll need to readjust the set on a regular basis. Some tape manufacturers also make test tapes for monitor adjustment.

KIT BAG

Some programs you produce will be done at your convenience and timing, but others will have tight deadlines. The latter events will prove Murphy's first law: "If anything can go wrong, it will." Begin to put together a kit bag of all the things you might possibly need for emergencies. Here's a beginning list:

Scissors (small and large), darning needles, safety pins of all sizes, plastic clothespins, small and large staplers, paper clips, razor blades or craft knives, nails in several sizes and a hammer, several colors of thread, screwdrivers (slot and phillips), asbestos gloves for handling hot bulbs, picture-hanging wire, small soldering iron, solder, tape measure, markers, fishing line, hacksaw, keyhole saw, small flashlight (you might blow a fuse), light rope, pliers, diagonal cutters, vise grip pliers, electrical tape. . . .

MAINTENANCE

Much of the maintenance on video equipment must be done by professionals, but you should learn how to clean the heads of your recorder. Some manuals suggest cleaning every 500 hours, while other professionals involved in critical work recommend cleaning heads before every use. Use only cleaner recommended for video heads. Alcohol and other solvents might affect the delicate parts. NEVER SWAB A HEAD IN THE VERTICAL DIRECTION. The head is extremely thin and could be broken loose from its mounting. Gently wipe across its gap horizontally. Repeat this process by gently moving the other head into a convenient position. Use the foam swabs supplied with the head cleaning chemical so that no lint or threads will be lodged in the head gaps. Clean the audio and "erase" heads as well.

A frequent cause of failure in small video systems is defective cables. They are subject to frequent handling, and the connectors are often of light-duty quality. Check cables first when your system seems to be malfunctioning. A few dollars invested in an inexpensive ohmmeter or continuity checker will be well spent. Cables can be quickly checked for open circuits or shorts. Be sure to test all inner conductors and the shield. Jiggle the wire while testing. If you are unfamiliar with this procedure, ask the service technician at your dealer's shop for the simple instructions. Handle all cables carefully. Do not bend video cables into a circle of less than 6 inches radius. Tape the points at which cables enter connectors to provide additional strain relief.

USING SLIDES

Pictures that look great on a projection screen do not always look good when recorded through a video camera. The TV camera has a much lower tolerance to contrast variations. Darker areas in a slide will be lost on the TV receiver as muddy black. Efforts to adjust the brightness at the camera or recorder will wash out the color in the rest of the picture. Choose slides with an overall even illumination. Avoid slides taken in bright outdoors with deep shadows. Since the inexpensive camera has limited resolving power, avoid materials with a lot of fine detail. Projector bulbs tend to be somewhat cooler than the lamps used in your lighting kit. Adjust the camera's color controls accordingly. By moving the camera smoothly across a projected slide, an interesting sense of motion can be added to still pictures. Move into the area of interest by panning, tilting, or zooming.

Keep your eyes and ears open, and use your imagination to discover other ways to compensate for your limited budget and space. At first your video equipment might be used as an expensive toy. Work hard to turn it into a useful tool.

8

Case Studies

The six case studies which follow are designed to show how NBV is being used in a variety of real-life situations. They represent use by small and large local congregations, regional organizations, and national groups.

Each person's or group's situation will differ, and these case studies may or may not fit your own circumstances. They are presented here to encourage you by showing groups that have seen a vision of the future and have wanted to make that vision a reality.

In almost every case the individuals involved began with only an idea and began to work on it. Most of them had little or no training in video before they began; yet each of them has been able to learn the language of the "New Pentecost" and speak it clearly and fluently.

Case Study No. 1
Videomission
American Baptist Churches of the Great Rivers Region

"Videomission" is the name given to the video project of American Baptist Churches of the Great Rivers Region. Several years ago Great Rivers saw the possibilities for NBV in the areas of mission interpretation and Christian education.

They purchased some close-out models of the Sony Betamax and a black-and-white camera and began to produce simple "talking-head" type tapes. These tapes and a playback machine were then delivered to individual churches by one of the area ministers. Visiting missionaries were the subject of most of the early tapes, and the popularity of the system began to grow.

Gradually color equipment was added, and one of the area ministers who had exhibited talent and interest was assigned to work 50 percent of his time on the project.

Today Videomission has a complete portable color studio that will fit in the trunk of a standard-sized car and can be used for any variety of remote or studio taping. The equipment includes two color cameras, a color portapak, a special effects generator, and a switcher. Portable lighting and audio equipment are included in the package. They have also purchased a Sony 3/4" editing setup and are using that to produce some very professional-looking tapes.

The popularity of this program is increasing with the churches, and a current catalog lists over one hundred tapes available on *any* format requested.

Playback machines are still delivered by the area ministers, but as the project grows, more and more churches are buying their own playback equipment.

The tapes are provided free of charge, the only cost to the user being return postage.

Programs are still heavily concentrated in the area of mission interpretation (interviews with missionaries on furlough, etc.), but the national staff of Educational Ministries of the ABC/USA has also been co-opted to produce teacher training tapes, and they have purchased the teacher training series called "The Other School System."

At a recent convention of the ABC/USA, one of the Videomission tapes demonstrated the power and intimacy that the proper use of video can bring to the churches' mission. The tape was a straightforward interview with one of the denomination's medical missionaries in India. At the end of the interview the interviewer held the missionary's hand and asked if they could pray together for the needs of the people the missionary worked with. As they prayed, slides of the mission field were shown on the screen. As this tape was played for groups of people who gathered around the TV set, a mood quickly developed that amazed even the producers of the tape. At the end of the tape, while the prayer was being said, members of the audience would invariably bow their heads and join in silent prayer with those on the tape. The audience was captured by the tape and became a part of the spiritual support for a missionary who was now several thousand miles away. It was an impressive sight.

Videomission's success has been so great that it has inspired other ABC churches and regions to get started in video. Every effort has been made to coordinate the purchase of equipment to minimize standardization problems and prevent the unnecessary duplication of production equipment.

For more information, write: Videomission, P.O. Box 3786, Springfield, IL 67208. Phone: (217) 525-1386.

Case Study No. 2
Ecclesia Productions
Muskegon, Michigan

Ecclesia Productions is a ministry of the First Baptist Church of Muskegon, Michigan. Using only volunteers, the church produces six weekly programs for the local cable system. These programs are done in behalf of the wider church community in Muskegon. Thirty volunteers are guided by a committee, but program producers have a wide latitude in their programming.

Originally started as a counterforce to commercial religious TV, the project quickly grew to a community-building device.

An initial investment of $25,000 was raised by the churches, and the Muskegon County Council of Churches provided an additional $1,000. In 1978, $12,000 was raised from a variety of community sources for editing equipment.

The programs produced are broadly ecumenical in spirit and implementation.

Programs include the regular worship service of First Baptist Church, although no pitch is made to invite viewers to come to that church. Other programs are designed for fundamentalist or Black viewers. The International Sunday School Lessons provide the basis for another series. A rotating series covers local religious personalities, churches, and children's programs.

The equipment is also available for developing noncable programming for use in church school and other settings.

For more information, write for the annual report of Ecclesia Productions from Rev. John Brown, First Baptist Church, 1070 S. Quarterline Rd., Muskegon, MI 49442.

Case Study No. 3
Riverside Church
New York City

When Riverside Church sold an AM radio station, some of the money was used to purchase some video equipment to send the Sunday service out on the local cable system. As interest grew, a volunteer staff of some forty individuals were trained and put to work on other cable programming. Volunteers are divided up among several "production units" and are supervised by a paid staff member of the church who gives about 20 percent of her time to the project.

The church has begun to produce tapes for in-house use as well, and the NBV/group media use is destined to become a major portion of the volunteers' work. Tapes include a fund-raising appeal, performances of the very active theater group, and a tape explaining some of the valuable tapestries hanging in the church.

Riverside Church is a huge operation, and the video equipment is invaluable in keeping one part of the congregation in touch with the others. Members of the church are able to share the joys and concerns of one group in a way that would not be possible through other media.

Emily Deeter, who oversees the video program, says they have about $60,00 invested in equipment and an annual operating budget of about $7,500. She thinks that it's best for a church to look into renting or leasing equipment first, purchasing it only after the program catches on.

For more information, write: Emily Deeter, Riverside Church, Riverside Drive and 122 St., New York, NY 10027.

Case Study No. 4
Baltimore Conference of the United Methodist Church

The Baltimore Conference of the United Methodist Church has been making video equipment available to its churches through its districts for several years.

The conference owns two portapaks, two ½" reel-to-reel recorders, and three studio cameras. They also have a portable switcher and a special effects generator. All of this is made available to district offices which can use this equipment for special projects, such as taping a training conference, and then the tape is made available to any of the other districts or churches which want it.

Three years ago they decided that one way to put video equipment into each of the five districts in the conference would be to offer matching grants of $750 towards the purchase of equipment. Each of the five districts came up with another $750, and each purchased a Panasonic black-and-white portapak unit.

Each district now makes the equipment available to the local churches for their use.

Ken Brown, who heads the program for the conference, says that about three churches per district use the equipment heavily, and perhaps twelve per district use it regularly. He indicated that perhaps fifty or sixty other churches have used it for one purpose or another.

Ken also has some observations about the use of video in the Baltimore Conference which may be true elsewhere. Ken has observed that it seems to be the smaller churches that are making the most extensive use of NBV. He's not sure why this might be the case but suspects that it may be that smaller churches tend to have younger pastors who are less afraid of the new technology. The younger pastors, he notes, have had more opportunities for learning video techniques in college and seminary. He also suggests that larger churches may be less impressed with video as a medium because they have a variety of other resources available to them.

Another interesting aspect of the Baltimore Conference's video program is that the local church people who have borrowed the equipment have shown remarkable creativity in their use of video and "have done the impossible because they didn't realize it was impossible."

Ken has also noticed that the laity seem to be a major driving force behind the use of video in the churches. More and more lay people are being trained in the use of the equipment, and they are coming into the district offices to borrow the equipment for a number of projects.

Ken sees a great deal of growth in the future for the use of NBV in the Baltimore Conference of the United Methodist Church and the wider church community as well, and he welcomes it. For more information, write to the Baltimore Conference of the United Methodist Church, 516 N. Charles St., Baltimore, MD 21201.

Case Study No. 5
Christ Lutheran Church
Kulpsville, Pennsylvania

Christ Lutheran Church in Kulpsville, Pennsylvania, has used video on a number of occasions, but their latest project is the most ambitious to date.

Borrowing black-and-white equipment from Lutheran Theological

Seminary in Mt. Airy (Philadelphia), the church developed a videotape entitled "The Greatest Story Ever Told—His Story." Designed as a stewardship tool, the tape tells how the Christ story is told through the congregation's life, work, and people.

The idea was to challenge the congregation to grow in its willingness to tell the story more effectively. It was hoped that the tape would help the church members see their role in the proclamation of the gospel, its implications in worship, and their financial responsibility for the church's attempt to "tell His story."

After the tape was finished, it was used in "cottage meetings" during a week-long commitment drive. Two players were used to play the tape in the homes of selected members where fifteen to twenty other members had been invited. After the tape was played, discussions were held about the message of the tape and its implications in the lives of the individuals present.

The church chose to use black-and-white equipment because of the availability of editing equipment in that format. Some of the taping was done with a two-camera system, but the majority was done with a single camera (film style) and edited later.

The pastor of the church, Richard Stephans, has had a few training sessions in video, but much of the work was done by two high school students who used skills learned in their classes at school.

The church has around five hundred members and has tried tape-slide programs of this sort before, but Reverend Stephans thinks this approach will be far more effective because of the immediacy and motion. The only cost to the church will be for two reels of tape for the master tapes used in the "cottage meetings." Any church can be pleased with a budget like that. For more information, write to Christ Lutheran Church, Sumneytown Pike, Kulpsville, PA 19443.

Case Study No. 6
Covenant Press Video
Chicago, Illinois

The Evangelical Covenant Church of America is one of the smaller denominations on the American scene. Yet with only 78,000 members and 560 churches it is supporting one of the most active and ambitious denominational projects in the use of NBV.

In 1977 they began a program which placed a video player within the reach of local churches which were clustered in groups of eight. They had already begun producing tapes as early as 1975 so that when the players were made available, the churches had something to use on them. Covenant Press Video was born and continues to work under the ECCA's Department of Publication.

A volunteer "video representative" was assigned to each of the clusters, and they were responsible for the promotion of the use of video. As with many programs which rely on volunteers, the results varied. Today, however, CPV has 160 titles in its catalog, and individual churches are being encouraged to buy their own playback equipment which will increase usage.

CPV offers a variety of plans for usage, including a type of membership plan where a church which pays $200 per year ($300 if it is not a member of ECCA) gets unlimited use of the tapes in the catalog. There is only a small handling fee. Other churches or groups which are not members may rent the tapes for fees which are usually based on the tapes' length and whether or not they are a part of a series. Outright purchase of the tapes is also possible, although this happens rarely.

Ted Ericson, who runs CPV, says that they are sending out 150 tapes a month, and one thing that seems to be of great value is the fact that any title can be sent to a church when they want it. Since copies of the originals are made up as they are requested (no inventory), there is no worry over conflicting dates as can happen in a conventional film library.

CPV offers their titles in all three major formats and is now emphasizing their use in the *home* so as to increase the flexibility of utilizations.

CPV has no "built-in studio" as such and prefers to go "on location" whenever possible. Most of their production equipment is rented to fit the needs of a given project. An increasing number of churches are purchasing camera and production equipment, and some of their tapes have found their way into the CPV catalog.

Ericson says that the denominational bureaucrats are now beginning to see the tremendous potential for NBV in their programs and are coming to him with ideas for tapes.

CPV has developed a funding strategy for these types of tapes by which a group who puts up money for the production of a tape, perhaps a mission interpretation tape of the work in Zaire, receives a royalty each time that tape is rented. This money is then placed into an "escrow" account which is then applied to the next production sponsored by the group. This has two beneficial results. First, it encourages the production of more tapes, and second, it encourages the sponsoring group to promote the use of the tape so that additional royalties will be earned, thereby enabling more productions.

For further information and a catalog, contact: Ted Ericson, Covenant Press Video, 3200 W. Foster Ave, Chicago, IL 60625. Phone: (312) 478-4676.

Appendixes

1

2

3

4

Appendix 1
Suggested Uses of NBV

A. CHRISTIAN EDUCATION

1. Videotape programs (or segments) off the TV set, such as *All in the Family, Maude,* Public Broadcasting Service specials, programs on hunger, racism, etc. Use these as discussion starters.
2. Introduce new curriculum via tape.
3. Let the church school teacher see himself or herself in action.
4. Record special resource persons, such as visiting theologians, evangelists, and others who lecture. Put this videotape in the "tape bank" for review and discussion later as well as for sharing with other churches, groups, etc.
5. Make instructional tapes, such as storytelling, use of bulletin board, hymnal, etc.
6. Create resource material presentations for classes to encourage participation and discussion.
7. Tape in-service training, such as lab schools, leadership seminars, etc., which everyone can't attend.
8. Teaching tool for groups.
9. Tape pastor's input to class when pastor is unable to be there in person.
10. Use in "interest centers" in church school.
11. Produce tape for use in home Bible study courses.
12. Bring various age groups together for intergenerational learning projects.

B. WORSHIP

1. Minister may use tape to rehearse sermon.
2. Use in counseling to reveal nonverbals.
3. Tape sermon and feedback discussion on the sermon with pastor not present.
4. Videotape sermon illustration: dramatic sketches, interviews.
5. Tape sermon for use in self-analysis.
6. Department worship analysis re: offering, Communion, acolytes, ushers, etc.
7. Preserve programs on Christmas, Easter, and other special times of the year.

8. Tape a wedding rehearsal; use as example to couples planning a wedding.
9. Choir director can let choir *see* as well as hear themselves.
10. In-service training for ushers, acolytes, etc.
11. Tape "a day in the life of your minister."

C. MEMBERSHIP DEVELOPMENT

1. For new members of a church, videotape a tour of the whole church, meet the staff, church school teachers, nursery attendant, etc.
2. Produce a program on what the church is doing. Use it in connection with every visitation/commitment program.
3. Take church to shut-ins and nursing homes via VTR; then videotape a message from the shut-ins back to the congregation.
4. Tape work of lay people in the church's activities.
5. Use VTR to develop speaking abilities of members.

D. EVANGELISM

1. Go into homes of prospective members and introduce them to congregations through VTR presentation (played back on their own TV set).
2. Prepare a tape explaining what your church believes, how it operates, etc., and place it on cable system.
3. Tape people relating what the gospel means to them.
4. Tape people telling how the church has helped in times of crisis.

E. YOUTH

1. Interest youth in Christian vocations via videotape interviews with lay people talking about their careers.
2. Tape children role-playing in the church school.
3. Record youth service fund projects.
4. Use VTR to help youth study "adult culture."
5. Youth can produce their own "TV commercials," using themes from the Bible or contemporary culture.

F. LIFE OF THE CHURCH

1. Videotape a "letter." (Example: One congregation, upset over a national decision, sent a videotape of this reaction to

national headquarters. A national official personally responded on videotape.)

2. Tape a play without memorization in small sections and edit together.
3. Put VTR equipment in hands of opposing groups. Have them present either point of view in a given amount of time. Let groups see an immediate playback of how they function, look, react to, and use nonverbal communication.
4. Book reviews (with illustrations, etc.).
5. Use VTR to put a confirmation class on the cable system.
6. Interview church members getting opinions regarding various programs.
7. Videotape "hot" issues in assembly sessions to present in local churches.
8. Use VTR to promote camp, assemblies, community activities, and other church programs.
9. Videotape a group functioning well in a sensitivity situation.
10. Use camera at eye level of a five-year-old to show what church looks like to this size person; sensitize adults to this perspective.

G. HISTORICAL

1. Encourage elders to reminisce on tape to preserve history of congregation.
2. Record historical events in life of church, such as groundbreaking, retirements, installations, dedications, etc.

H. ECUMENICAL

1. Record a Jewish sabbath service or a Roman Catholic mass, or different Protestant services to use in studying other faiths.
2. In larger parish situations, take VTR into each of the churches and show what life of other churches in the parish is like. (Contrast inner city/suburban, city/rural, etc.)
3. Use VTR to record ecumenical discussions for later study.

I. COMMUNITY INVOLVEMENT

1. Interview neighborhood/community people about community needs, etc.
2. Tape projects in your area for promotion and greater understanding.

3. Tape community concerns, such as traffic hazards, trash pick-up, community facility prejudice, etc., for various uses.
4. Offer use of the video equipment to others in the community (after they have been trained in its use).
5. Produce VTR public service announcements for use on cable TV systems.

APPENDIX 2
PRINTED MATERIAL ON NBV

PERIODICALS

Educational and Industrial Television. Monthly magazine on industrial and educational uses of TV. One of the best publications in the field. $15 per year. Write: C. S. Tepfer Publishing Co., P.O. Box 565, Ridgefield, CT 06877.

ITA News Digest. Publication of the International Tape Association. Covers all aspects of video and audio recording. Write: ITA, 10 W. 66th Street, New York, NY 10023. Phone: (212) 787-0910 for details.

Spectrum. Magazine written from evangelical Christian viewpoint to acquaint concerned Christians with what's happening in media. In-depth articles on all forms of media. For sample copy, write: Billy Graham Program in Communications, Wheaton College, Wheaton, IL 60187.

The Video Home Market. Survey conducted by *Time* magazine and distributed by the International Tape Association in their ITA News Digest (May-June, 1979). This is a very valuable resource for those planning to get into video, as it gives an indication of the widespread acceptance of this new medium. Write: ITA, 10 W. 66th Street, New York, NY 10023, for a copy.

The Videophile. Consumer-oriented bimonthly magazine. Excellent articles on equipment, legal issues, advertisements. Very current. $10 for six issues. Write: 2003 Appalachee Parkway, Tallahassee, FL 32301.

Video Cassette and CATV Newsletter. Helpful analyses of trends in NBV industry. Monthly. $48 per year. Write: P.O. Box 5254, Beverly Hills, CA 90210.

Videography. News and evaluative articles on video hardware and software from the industrial standpoint. Slick format. Monthly. $12 per year. Write: United Business Publications, 750 Third Avenue, New York, NY 10017.

Videoscope. Deals with sources of videotape information. Quarterly. $9.50 per year. Write: Gordon & Breach, 1 Park Avenue, New York, NY 10016.

Vid News. Digest of items on video developments from industry view-point. Biweekly. $45 per year. Write: United Business Publications, Inc., 750 Third Avenue, New York, NY 10017.

VU Marketplace. Articles and classified ads on variety of video topics. Heavy emphasis on NBV. $20 for 24 issues. Write: Knowledge Industry Publications, 2 Corporate Park Drive, White Plains, NY 10604.

BOOKS

Albright, David, *A Group Process and Videotape Workbook*. Lake Oswego, Oreg.: United Methodist Church, n.d. Using videotape as a tool to aid group process and involvement. Some unique concepts, such as a "hands off" approach. Emphasizes people involvement rather than hardware. 62 pages (with work and information sheets). $7.50. Write: United Methodist Church, 1855 S. Shore Boulevard, Lake Oswego, OR 97034.

Barwick, John, and Kranz, Stewart, *The Complete Videocassette Users Guide*. White Plains, N.Y.: Knowledge Industry Publications, 1973. An introduction to videocassettes and modeling of how they can be used. Includes organizations doing programming and a selection of existing programs. One of very few books dealing with programming in this medium. 169 pages. $29.50. Write: Knowledge Industry Publications, 2 Corporate Park Drive, White Plains, NY 10604.

——————————, *Profiles in Video: Who's Using Television and How*. White Plains, N.Y.: Knowledge Industry Publications, 1975. Case studies and reference guide to organizations using video communications (industry, government, education, medical). Programming applications that can be helpful to other organizations. 181 pages. $29.50.

Bensinger, Charles, *The Video Guide* (2d ed.). Santa Barbara, Calif.: Video-Info Publications, 1979. This is another complete guide for the beginner or more advanced user of video. Simple diagrams explain the technology of video. Good introductory chapters. It is available from Esselte Video, Inc., Order Center, Department 100, P. O. Box 978, Edison, NJ 08817. Ask for Stock #500 ($14.95 plus 75 cents for postage).

Editors of *Videography* Magazine, *The Video Handbook* (3d ed.). New York: United Business Publications, 1977. Basic reference manual for video production. Includes latest technologies, charts, glossary, and "Corporate Communications Centers Guide." Chapters on software, production studies, selecting equipment, etc. 128 pages. $12.75. Write: United Business Publications, 750 Third Avenue, New York, NY 10017.

Efrein, Joel, *Cablecasting Production Handbook*. Blue Ridge Summit, Pa.: Tab Books, 1975. A fairly technical overview of cable production for producers, educators, librarians. For those somewhat experienced, not beginners. 210 pages. $12.95.

Harwood, Don, *Everything You Always Wanted to Know About Video Tape Recording*. Bayside, N.Y.: VTR Publishing Co., 1974. Question-and-answer format on videotape production, editing, etc. 180 pages. $3.95.

Kalba, Kas, *Video Implosion: Models for Reinventing Television*. Palo Alto, Calif.: Aspen Institute Program on Communications and Society, n.d. An overview of video as an art form with models for community development education and alternative movements. Theoretical approach with working examples. $2. Write: Aspen Institute Program on Communications and Society, 770 Welch Road, Palo Alto, CA 94304.

Knecht, Kenneth B., *Designing and Maintaining the CATV and Small TV Studio* (2d ed.). Blue Ridge Summit, Pa.: Tab Books, 1976. A "how to" handbook for setting up, operating, and maintaining your own studio. Done in simple but detailed terms. Provides three system examples. 288 pages. $12.95.

Kybett, Harry, *The Complete Handbook of Videocassette Recorders*. Blue Ridge Summit, Pa.: Tab Books, 1977. A softcover book that gives a complete overview of technical aspects of the home video recorder. A must for those contemplating purchase of this equipment. 275 pages. $5.95.

Lachenbruch, David, *Video Cassette Recorders: The Complete Home Guide*. New York: Everest House, Publishers, 1979. This softcover book was written by one of the most knowledgeable writers in video today. This is a readable and comprehensive book for the video novice.

Mattingly, Grayson, and Smith, Welby, *Introducing the Single Camera VTR System: A Layman's Guide to Videotape Recording*. New York: Charles Scribner's Sons, 1973. A lay person's guide to videotape recording. Invaluable resource. A basic introduction primer. 150 pages. $8.95.

Murray, Michael, *The Videotape Book*. New York: Bantam Books, Inc., 1975. Paperback handbook for videotape production (mainly portapak). 248 pages. $1.95.

Robinson, Richard, *The Video Primer: Equipment, Production and Concepts*. New York: Music Sales Corporation, 1974. A sophisticated resource on VTR use. Extensive glossary. Brief bibliography. 380 pages. $7.95.

"Videofreex," *The Spaghetti City Video Manual*. New York: Praeger Publishers, Inc., 1973. An easy-to-read book on videotape equipment. Basically a repair and maintenance manual, though in clever format. $7.95.

Zettl, Herbert, *Television Production Handbook*. Belmont, Calif.: Wadsworth Publishing Co., Inc., 1976. A little dated but good basic TV production handbook.

Other Books About Television

Aiken, E. G. M., *Sound with Vision*. New York: Crane, Russak & Co., Inc., 1973.

Bachman, John W., *The Church in the World of Radio and Television*. Wilton, Conn.: Association Press, 1960.

Benson, Dennis, *Electric Evangelism: How to Spread the Word Through Radio and TV*. Nashville: Abingdon Press, 1973.

Chester, Giraud, et al., *Television and Radio*. New York: Appleton-Century-Crofts, 1971.

Clarke, Beverly, *Graphic Design in Educational Television*. New York: Watson-Guptill Publications, 1974.

Diamant, Lincoln, ed., *The Broadcast Communications Dictionary*. New York: Hastings House, Publishers, Inc., 1974.

Efrein, Joel, *Video Tape Production and Communication Techniques*. Blue Ridge Summit, Pa.: Tab Books, 1970.

Hilliard, Robert L., *Writing for Television and Radio*. New York: Hastings House, Publishers, Inc., 1962, 1973.

Jones, Peter, *The Techniques of the Television Cameraman*. New York: Hastings House, Publishers, Inc., 1974.

Millerson, Gerald, *The Technique of Lighting for Television and Motion*

Pictures. New York: Hastings House, Publishers, Inc., 1972.

_____, *The Technique of Television Production*. New York: Hastings House, Publishers, Inc., 1968.

_____, *Basic TV Staging*. New York: Hastings House, Publishers, Inc., 1974.

Nisbett, Alex, *The Use of Microphones*. New York: Hastings House, Publishers, Inc., 1975.

Oringel, Robert S., *Audio Control Handbook*. New York: Hastings House, Publishers, Inc., 1972.

Quick, John, and Wolff, Herbert, *Small Studio Video Tape Production*. Reading, Mass.: Addison-Wesley Publishing Co., Inc., 1972.

Robinson, Joseph, *Videotape Recording*. New York: Hastings House, Publishers, Inc., 1975.

Schwartz, Tony, *The Responsive Chord*. New York: Doubleday & Co., Inc., 1974.

Stasheff, Edward, and Bretz, Rudy, *The Television Program: Its Direction and Production*. New York: Hill & Wang, 1951, 1962.

Veith, Richard, *Talk-Back TV: Two-Way Cable Television*. Blue Ridge Summit, Pa.: Tab Books, 1976.

Zettl, Herbert, *Sight, Sound, Motion: Applied Media Aesthetics*. Belmont, Calif.; Wadsworth Publishing Co., Inc., 1973.

_____, *Television Production Handbook*. Belmont, Calif.: Wadsworth Publishing Co., Inc., 1968.

ARTICLES

"Television Enters the 80s," *New York Times Magazine* (August 19, 1979). This is a very comprehensive article on the future of both broadcast and nonbroadcast TV.

Time (October 30, 1978). Advertising supplement to this issue has excellent overview of the new home video systems and their applications.

"TV of Tomorrow," *Newsweek* (July 3, 1978). Extensive look at the coming revolution in video and home communications in general. Very good.

US News & World Report (June 26, 1978). Good overview of new video techniques and equipment.

"Video Cassette Recorders—Here Comes the Second Generation," *TV Guide* (October 28, 1978). Good summary of some of the latest developments in home recorders.

CATALOGS

Audio-Visual Equipment Directory. Published by National Audio-Visual Association. This is a pictorial catalog of all types of AV equipment, including TV. Write: NAVA, 3150 Spring St., Fairfax, VA 22031. Phone: (707) 273-7200 for information and price.

Citizens Media Directory, The. Lists almost 400 national and local media reform groups, public access centers, video groups. $7.50. Write: National Citizens Committee for Broadcasting, 1530 P. St., N.W., Washington, DC 20005.

Comprehensive Video Supply Corporation. Write: 148 Veterans Drive, Northvale, NJ 07647 for catalog.

Episcopal Church Video Resource Guide, The. Lists video programming produced in the Episcopal Church and from other selected sources. It includes synopsis of programs, equipment information, and model programs. Available from EDSO Video, 412 Sycamore St., Cincinnati, OH 45202. $35.

Illustrated Trade Reference. Religious media discount buying service. Write: Quality Media Corporation, Suite 1A, 825 Indian Trail Road, Destin, FL 32541.

ITA Source Directory. Complete listing of hardware manufacturers, software producers, etc. Write: ITA, 10 W. 66th Street, New York, NY 10023, on letterhead stationery for free copy. Additional copies are $1 each.

Video Bluebook, The. A guide to program suppliers and video services—especially for business, industry, and government video users. One of the best guides of this kind, though expensive. 350 pages. $29.50. Write: Knowledge Industry Publications, 2 Corporate Park Drive, White Plains, NY 10604.

Video Log—Programs of Interest and Entertainment, The. This is a fully annotated catalog with entries on over 4,500 programs. There is a subject index. Also available from Esselte Video, Order Center, Department 100, P. O. Box 978, Edison, NJ 08817. Order Stock #300 ($20).

Videoplay Program Source Guide. Listing of video program suppliers who distribute in 3⁄4″ video cassette format, as of 1974. $2.50. Write: C. S. Tepfer Publishing Co., P. O. Box 565, Ridgefield, CT 06877.

Video Programs/Index. 1978 (3d annual edition). Sources for commercial video programming (entertainment, instruction, training). Identified by subject categories and format (e.g., 1⁄2″ Betamax). Includes a number of cross-referenced indices (fee use, off-air recording). $3. Write: Video Programs/Index, 923 Sixth Street, S.W., Washington, DC 20024.

APPENDIX 3
SUPPLIERS OF PRERECORDED TAPES FOR NBV

COVENANT PRESS VIDEO: This small denomination has one of the largest video libraries in the country. Over 160 titles are available. See Case Study No. 6 for a description of the project. Write them at 320 W. Foster Ave., Chicago, IL 60625, or phone (312) 478-4676 for a catalog.

CRS VIDEO: Church Resource Systems has a number of video programs available for sale and rental. They concentrate on the area of leadership development. Write: CRS Video, P. O. Box 990, Dallas, TX 75221.

DAYTON ELECTROMEDIA WORKSHOP: This is a project of United Methodist groups in the area of Dayton, Ohio. It provides tapes of Christian music concerts and other programming on 3/4" or 1/2" tape. Write: Rev. Raymond L. Wiblin, Dayton Electromedia Workshop, % United Theological Seminary, 1810 Harvard Boulevard, Dayton, OH 45406.

EPISCOPAL RADIO-TV FOUNDATION: Twelve-session course called "What Think Ye of Jesus?", a look at the historical Jesus. Rev. John Stone Jenkins is the teacher. This is the first offer by the foundation on video, and they plan many more. Write them at 3379 Peachtree Road, N.E., Atlanta, GA 30326, to get their catalog and have your name put on their mailing list.

NATIONAL INSTITUTE OF BIBLICAL STUDIES, INC.: This group leases a series of lectures by biblical scholars to those who want to set up a lay seminary or Bible college. Generally a "talking head" format but very well produced. Write: NIBS, 4001 N. Dixie Highway, #204, Pompano Beach, FL 33064, for sample tape and printed information. Phone: (305) 781-4650.

PUBLIC TELEVISION LIBRARY: A department of the Public Broadcasting Service. This is a library of programs that have been broadcast on public television. Rental and purchase and rights to reduplicate are available. Write: The Public Television Library, 475 L'Enfant Plaza, S.W., Washington, DC 20024, for catalog and price information. Phone: (202) 488-5220.

TELEVISION UN-BROADCAST EXPERIENCE (TUBE): Write the

Division of Communication, American Baptist Churches in the U.S.A., Valley Forge, PA 19481, to be placed on a monthly mailing list that describes the current offerings of interviews with Christians from around the world involved in the ongoing ministry of the church.

TIME-LIFE MULTIMEDIA: Library of video resources. Includes "The Long Search" series on world religions. Write: Time-Life Multimedia, Time-Life Building, New York, NY 10020, for catalog and price information.

VIDEOMISSION: Dan Holland, coordinator. This is the video library of the American Baptist Churches of the Great Rivers Region. It contains over seventy videotapes available on any format. Most are about ABC mission fields, but they also have some training tapes of interest to Christian educators. Write: Dan Holland, P. O. Box 3786, Springfield, IL 62708, for catalog. Phone: (217) 525-1386.

This list will continue to grow as we all learn of more sources of prerecorded tapes that could be of use to a religious audience. If you know of other sources, please write: Terry Vaughn, Division of Communication, American Baptist Churches in the U.S.A., Valley Forge, PA 19481. Phone: (215) 768-2305.

APPENDIX 4
SOURCES OF VIDEOTAPE EQUIPMENT

Unfortunately, most churches and community groups do not have videotape equipment. Videotape equipment is expensive. A basic ½" open-reel (black-and-white) videotape recorder, camera, and playback monitor package will cost around $2,500 or more. Color equipment can more than double this amount.

Unfortunately, most churches and other groups do not want to invest in such equipment until they have had an opportunity to see how they could use it and how their membership will derive benefits from it.

Fortunately, there are several possible ways for you to have access to video equipment. This will enable you to become familiar with it, to see how easy it is to operate, and to evaluate the results obtained.

The first thing to remember is that playback equipment is usually more readily available than recording equipment. There is a growing amount of material available on videotape; so let's take a look at sources for playback equipment first.

A number of school systems as well as colleges and universities have extensive videotape systems. If an individual school does not have some, check at their city or district audiovisual office.

Don't forget to check with the cable TV system in your area. Often they have such equipment for loan or rental at a modest fee.

Some larger municipal libraries, as well as some museums, have video equipment. Don't overlook these possibilities.

Of course, there is always the chance that another church in your area might have some video equipment.

Another possibility is the commercial audiovisual dealer(s) in your area. Most are willing to set up a demonstration of their equipment for your church, ministerial association, council of churches, etc. Often they have trade-in equipment which is considerably less expensive. If the dealer can offer a warranty on this equipment, you can get into the "videotape business" with much less investment.

Videotape recorders and cameras can be a little more difficult to obtain. The results you can get with their use make the extra effort well worthwhile.

The best sources for a video camera and VTR are schools, colleges, universities, medical centers, museums, or similar facilities. Industries are using video in a significant way. Over two hundred national and regional corporations have staff working full-time in the area of video. Training and orientation are the two principle areas, but public relations and sales are not far behind. Remember also the cable TV system and the commercial video products dealer as additional sources, although rental is probably their answer to your inquiry.

Glossary
of Video Terms

This glossary will in no way attempt to cover all of the terms and technical definitions of the video industry. It will, however, describe in as nontechnical a way as possible the kinds of words you will find in the operating manuals of your equipment. As you read more widely in trade journals or texts on television production, you will be confronted by a plethora of video jargon which will drive you to a much more complete glossary, but the following pages should help in your use of this book.

A

Aperture. This is a term common to photography as well as video. It refers to the opening in the lens which varies the amount of light allowed to affect the picture tube. The aperture is controlled by a ring on the barrel of the lens marked in f-stop numbers. The maximum opening will usually be about f2, while the minimum will be f16 or f22. The f will not appear on the ring. Each number represents half or twice the amount of light of the number next to it.

Aspect Ratio. This refers to the proportions of the TV picture, and this ratio is 4 units wide by 3 units high. This is important for you to know, since the aspect ratio of 35-mm slides is 6 units wide by 4 units high. Slides shot for particular use in your TV productions should keep important details away from the edges.

Assemble Edit. An assemble edit is one which adds one program segment after another on a tape, laying down new control track, sound, and video with each section. High-quality editors will make the change during the vertical interval when the scanning beam is retracing to start a new picture.

Audio Head. The audio head in a VTR is several inches downstream from the video head drum. The control track head is usually a part of this same housing. As the tape passes by a very narrow gap, a tiny electrical field in the head induces changes in the oxide of the videotape. Your main concern with this head will be a regularly scheduled gentle cleaning with the proper materials.

Audio Mixer. This may be a "passive" or "active" sound controller which is used to vary and mix the volume of microphones and other sound sources, such as phonographs and cassette tape recorders. A passive mixer simply inhibits the signal with some variable resistance. These mixers are inexpensive but hardly satisfactory for your purposes. A good active mixer will amplify the voltages from microphones and match the input to your recorder properly. There's a wide variation in price and features. Better-quality equipment will be hum-free, will allow mixing of several kinds of sound sources, and will have a good meter for setting proper levels.

Automatic Gain or Level Control (AGC or ALC). Very few, if any, 1/2" VCRs have user-adjustable volume controls. An electronic circuit measures the sound level at its input and raises or lowers it to an optimum level. This means one less knob to worry about, but it also means that the machine tries to make everything you do sound the same. Try out this feature on the equipment you are considering for purchase.

Automatic Light Control. This does to video signals what AGC does to sound. The disadvantage is that bright sky or a backlight behind your center of action will cause the camera to lower its sensitivity and darken the whole scene. More elaborate cameras have override switches. The alternative for cheaper cameras is to avoid backlighted situations.

B

Barn Doors. These metal flaps can be mounted by means of a frame to a reflector to control the way in which light falls on a scene.

Black Level. A true black on a television tube is produced by a minimum signal rather than no signal at all. This voltage has an industry-recommended level for cameras. Less expensive cameras will probably have an internal adjustment for this black, set-up, or pedestal level (all three terms are used). When it's out of adjustment, picture contrast will suffer.

Brightness Ratio. If you plan to use slides in your productions, you will need to be concerned about the difference between the lightest and the darkest areas in a scene. A very contrasty picture will not reproduce well on TV. Scenes shot outdoors in bright sun can also have very high contrast in shadow areas. Watch out for hats, shadows from buildings, trees, etc.

C

Capstan. A very carefully machined shaft in a recorder which moves at a carefully controlled speed to move the tape through the tape track. Tape is held against the capstan by the rubber pinch roller.

Capstan Servo Editing. In a high quality recorder, the capstan motor has circuitry which constantly checks the control signals coming from the source recorder or camera and varies the tape speed so that the tape being edited is always in exact synchronization with the source program being added to it. By this means, when the switch from one program to another is made, there is no disruption of picture or control track information. This is a very desirable feature in a recorder and is necessary for true electronic editing.

Cardioid. Refers to the heart-shaped sensitivity pattern of a particular kind of microphone. Sound waves coming from the rear and sides are rejected to a measurable degree.

Chroma keying. This is a special effect used in professional television to replace the background in one scene with a new scene. News-casters are suddenly seen sitting in front of the scene about which they are talking. An actress advertising a product moves from apartment to street to airport. The actor stands in front of a blue (generally) background, and special circuits replace all blue that is seen by that camera with the signal from a second source. This is one of the most useful visual devices in television.

Chrominance. The saturation of color or the hue of a particular scene as differentiated from the brightness.

Close-up. This is a camera angle of view which shows the subject in some detail. With persons as the subject, a close-up shot will include the head only.

C-mount. Most small video cameras use *C*-mount lenses. This refers to the threaded barrel which fastens the lens to the camera. This lens mounting system is also common to 16-mm movie cameras, and this provides for easy interchangeability. Used 16-mm lenses can often be obtained for closeup videotaping of pictures and table-top scenes.

Coaxial Cable. The single-conductor shielded cable which is used to carry high frequency signals between pieces of equipment. Be advised, however, that there is some loss in signal strength over long cable runs. Amplifiers may be needed if your installation calls for the interconnection of rooms or buildings more than 500 feet apart.

Color Bars. These are electronically produced bars of standard colors placed usually at the beginning of a videotape to aid in the adjustment of the receivers or monitors.

Control Track. The track of synchronizing pulses placed along one edge of a videotape which is used to keep the various parts of the recorder timed properly. When this track is disturbed, the picture will break up, and you'll hear the head drive motor going through wide fluctuations in speed.

Cookie. A screen with a random or regular design pattern of holes. This is placed in front of a background light to cast shadows on a part of the scene—usually a plain background that needs a touch of variety added.

Crash edit. This is an edit made without any regard to the vertical interval or control track of the end tape. A "dry" or "passive" switcher will make such an edit as you switch from one camera to another. The picture will "glitch" or tear until synchronization is reestablished. If such edits must be made, fade the camera to black first.

Cross Pulse Generator. This is a circuit which changes the timing of the television signal so that the control pulses, which are normally not seen, appear in the middle of the screen. Such a circuit is often incorporated into a high-quality monitor which can be attached to a videotape recorder. The cross pulse signals can be used to monitor several operating parameters, including proper tape tension, color control signal, and head-switching problems.

D

Demodulation. The process of stripping picture and sound information from the broadcast or carrier signal transmitted by a TV station (or modulator in a VTR). The demodulated signal can then be processed by the picture and sound circuits of the TV set or monitor.

DIN. This stands for *Deutsche Industrie-Norm,* or "German Industrial Standard." Some audio equipment uses these barrel-shaped plugs with three to six inner pins.

Dolly Wheels. Are usually connected to a folding spiderlike arrangement which can be fastened to the feet of a tripod. This also refers to the action of moving the camera toward or away from the scene. A director's instruction might be, "Dolly in slowly."

Dubbing. This refers to copying from a master tape to make copies or replacing audio already on the tape with new audio. Many recorders have an "audio dub" control which permits replacing audio without disturbing the picture.

E

ECU (Extreme Close-Up). Generally the face or even just a part of the face of an actor.

Editing Equipment. Some VTRs have special electronic circuits which allow smooth insertion of new segments into an existing program (see "insert edit" and "assemble edit"). Several manufacturers have sophisticated control consols available which will allow automatic operation of two or more VTRs for very precise editing. The point at which an edit is made is located by a time counter which translates the control track pulses on the tape into a time readout. In some elaborate machines, this time code is permanently recorded on one of the sound tracks and can be manipulated through computer-assisted controls. The precise edit point is determined on both the original material and the resulting edited tape. The editing controller will automatically back up both machines approximately five seconds and then automatically switch at the precise edit point during the vertical interval.

Electret. This is a type of sensitive microphone which requires battery power to operate.

Electronic Editing. Usually refers to the sophisticated assembling or inserting of new material on a tape without disturbing the control tracks, as opposed to crash edits.

ENG. This is a term you'll see in catalogs in which the various features of portable cameras and recorders are described. It means "electronic news gathering" and also refers to a single-camera style of recording, similar to using a movie camera.

Establishing Shot. Often the first shot of a sequence, chosen to give the viewer a point of view to establish the setting.

F

Fade. To change the strength of an audio or video signal so that the picture or sound fades in or out. A simple fade to or from black can be accomplished by starting the VTR with the camera iris closed and opening to the optimum *f*-stop with the recorder running. A fade to black, using the camera iris, is the revese of this process.

Floor Director. The person who gives hand signals at the direction of the director who is usually not in sight. The floor director, as the name implies, is on the studio floor during tapings.

Field. The signal which causes the flying electron spot to make one pass over the screen. Two fields interlace to make one frame of 525 lines.

Film Chain. This is a special movie projector which is coupled to a television camera to place movies on the TV screen. A film chain in a studio will usually have several sources, such as slide and movie projectors able to feed one camera. Some companies make relatively inexpensive devices to use slide projectors, 16- and 8-mm projectors, with lower cost television cameras.

First Generation. Each time a video signal is transferred from one tape to another, it loses a generation. The original recording is the first generation. There is a limit to the number of times a program can be "aged" before its quality suffers dramatically.

Fluid Head. This type of tripod head uses a bed of fluid between the mounting plates so that very smooth operation is possible. This type of equipment can be a real boon to a single-camera operation.

Foot Candles. A foot candle is a measure of the amount of light falling on an area. While many cameras will operate satisfactorily at low-light levels, manufacturers' literature often suggests a minimum of 140-foot candles. Some photographic light meters are calibrated in foot candles and can be used to check your scene lighting.

Frame. One complete television picture consisting of 525 lines. In the North American system, there are thirty frames scanned every second.

F-Stop. Television camera lenses are marked in the same manner as photographic lenses. The f-stop is the measure of the size of lens in relation to its focal length. The smaller f-stop numbers set the lens iris to allow more light to pass through. As the f numbers increase, the iris is stopped down.

G

Gain. Refers to the amount of amplification of a signal and is a term used in both video and audio terminology. Gain is often specified in "db" or decibels. This term is a definition of relative signal strength derived from a fairly complicated formula.

Glitch. A breakup of the picture seen as an ascending horizontal bar. This is caused by noise disturbance or momentary loss of synchronizing information. In a closed circuit system, noise can come from fluorescent lights, motors, etc.

Graphics. A term applied to all artwork and lettering. It can be used of anything on a flat surface like poster board, etc.

Gobo. This is a decorative or functional frame through which the television picture is shot for special effects. In a single-camera system, a title card may have a window cut in it toward which the camera might move and eventually encompass the whole scene beyond.

Gray Scale. These steps from black to white are often produced electronically or printed on a card to determine how faithfully a camera can reproduce the luminance spectrum. Gray scales are also used to balance three-tube television cameras.

Grid. Studio and theater lighting is usually suspended from a gridwork of pipes. It is often convenient, if a room will be used for video over a period of time, to build a simple light grid and acquire the appropriate clamps and fittings.

H

Halo. This is a warning sign that your camera pickup tube may be in danger of being burned by a too-bright light source. This appears as a black area around a bright point of light. Avoid aiming your camera at bright lights or especially directly into the sun. Reflections from mirrors or chrome can also cause problems.

Head Alignment. Refers to the proper positioning of the video, audio, and erase heads in a recorder so that they will scan the magnetic lines of information accurately.

Helical Scan Recording. This is the system common to all the 1/2" and 3/4" VTRs. Either the head drum or the tape path is canted at a slight angle so that as the tape passes around the drum, the rotating heads scribe a long diagonal line from one edge of the tape to the other.

Hertzian Waves. All the waves of the radio type; named for Heinrich Hertz who discovered the principle of transmission of radio waves.

Horizontal Resolution. The evaluation of the number of vertical lines from a test pattern that can be seen in a horizontal direction on the monitor screen. This then becomes a comparative measure of video equipment's ability to produce sharp pictures.

Horizontal Sync. These pulses control the scanning of the TV picture lines across the face of the tube or the camera. This circuit is regulated by the 60-cycle a/c which also powers the equipment.

I

Image Retention. This is also called lag. Less expensive types of television pickup tubes have a tendency to hold the image on the target area for a period of time after the image source has been removed. Some adverse conditions can even cause a permanent image to be burned into the face of the tube, and this will always appear as a part of your picture. Follow your camera operating instructions closely to avoid this problem. Test several manufacturers' cameras for the least image retention.

Insert Edit. This type of editing is done electronically so that new information is added, replacing existing video, without disturbing the control track. At the end of the insert a "cutout" is accomplished where the switch back to the original program is also done in vertical interval.

IPS. Inches per second.

K

Keying. This is one of the most elaborate effects in television. The output of two or more cameras is combined to form a composite picture. The picture from one source will be filled into the lines of the second picture wherever the level of the second picture goes above a predetermined level. A shape such as a logo can be defined by a third camera. This can be inserted into an area in the picture from camera #1, while the picture from camera #2 will fill in the shape defined by camera #3. See "chroma keying" for additional information.

Keylight. The main source of light on a scene, often a spotlight set to emphasize the important subject(s) of that scene.

Keystone. The distortion caused by incorrect alignment between a projector and a screen. This most often appears in rooms where the projector is at a much lower level than the screen. When using slides with a video camera, keep the camera as close to the projector as possible and keep the projector in a horizontal plane.

L

Lag. A ghost image which is retained on the screen, usually because of insufficient light.

Lavaliere Mike. Refers to the many types of small microphones which are designed to be suspended from a cord around the neck. When properly used, they are one of the best types of mikes for lectures and interviews.

Lens Speed. This is a reference to a lens's ability to gather light and is expressed as its lowest f-stop number. Several factors enter into making a lens "fast," such as the size of the front optics, quality of glass, number and size of internal elements, and coating. Lenses should be evaluated in terms of their quality as well as speed. It is important that zoom lenses stay in focus through their focal length range.

Line Matching Transformer. These small audio devices are used to match microphones to mixers and amplifiers. Microphones will generally be low or high impedance (z) and may be switchable. Mixer inputs may be low or high, balanced or unbalanced, and are often switchable. In small, nonprofessional systems the major concern will be in a proper match. Low impedance equipment should be used when cables will be more than 15 feet long. Balanced, low impedance lines are generally used in professional installations.

Luminance. The level of brightness. The luminance signal is that voltage which changes at the output of the camera or other piece of video equipment as the brightness value of the picture changes. In color television, this signal controls the amount of color, while the chrominance signal controls the tint (the mix of red, green, and blue).

M

Master Monitor. This is a very high quality TV viewing device with very accurate color registration and excellent picture fidelity. These are often used by studios to monitor the quality of the picture being produced.

Matching Transformer. This small device is used to match 75-ohm coaxial cable to 300-ohm twin lead. One will often be needed to connect an antenna to the VTR and the output of the VTR to a TV set's antenna terminals.

Medium Shot. Camera angle between a close-up and long shot, usually the head and shoulders of the subject.

Mistracking. This is a condition which arises when there is improper head-to-tape contact. The displayed picture will be erratic and noisy.

Modulation. The process of adding one signal to another. Usually this refers to the adding of sound and picture signals to a broadcastable carrier.

Monitor. A TV set without any receiving circuitry limited to displaying video information from a recorder, VTR, or other video source. It may or may not have a sound amplifier and speaker.

Monitor/Receiver. A TV set capable of handling standard broadcasts or video information through the use of control switches. These devices will generally have an output for the received "off-the-air" signal so that it can be recorded by a VTR without a separate tuner. A monitor/receiver can be a good way for the beginning user to expand at a later date.

N

Neutral Density Filter. This is a photographic-type filter which reduces the amount of lens reaching the picture tube of the camera without affecting color. These filters are needed when using sensitive cameras in bright, outdoor situations.

Noise. Any unwanted signal in either video or audio is considered to be noise. In video circuits, noise can be interference of one signal with another, or the background random signals which become obvious when the video signal is too weak to blank them out. Noise is inherent to tape and electronic components at almost every stage of the recorder. Absence of noise is a measure of quality.

NTSC Color. The National Television Standards Committee established the North American system by which color signals are compatible for black-and-white reception.

O

Omnidirectional. Refers to a microphone which has a uniform pickup pattern in all directions. Unless your recording areas have good sound treatment or you have particular needs for this kind of sound pickup, you will probably find that unidirectional mikes are more useful.

Overscan. Television receivers are designed to show less than the full picture as seen by the TV camera. This overscan is designed to be about 8 percent, but it is often greater. For this reason, there is a "safe-action" and "safe-title" area which is well inside the edges of the picture as seen by the camera.

P

Panning. The process of turning the camera to the left or right. It comes from the word "panorama" which is to view a scene by turning through the whole 360°-circle of view.

Passive Mixer. Many inexpensive mixers are of this type. The output of the microphone is controlled by varying a resistance. The total output is less than the sum of all the inputs. This is generally not a wise investment for even amateur recording.

Patch Cord. A cable with a connector at each end for connecting different pieces of equipment. Invest in good quality cables. They are generally one of the weakest links in your system because of the constant hard use.

Peak White. This is the brightest part of the TV picture and should not exceed a standard voltage level, or else overall picture quality will suffer. These adjustments on a camera should only be changed by experienced persons with proper test instruments.

Pedestal. The blackest part of the picture is not at zero level but is at a standard voltage level. When misadjusted, picture contrast will suffer. Adjustment should be by instruments.

Phase. The proper adjustment of phase becomes critical in multiple-camera systems, since the phase of a color signal determines its hue. Phase is a measure of relative timing—signals are in-phase or out-of-phase by degrees (e.g., 5 degrees, 30 degrees). When you adjust the "tint" control of a TV set, you are changing the timing of the color signal in relation to other parts of the signal.

Pinch Roller. This is the rubber idler wheel which presses the tape against the accurately machined capstan so that it will be pulled through the tape track. Pinch rollers should be cleaned on a regular schedule along with other parts of the recorder.

Processing Amplifier. This piece of sophisticated equipment is used by professionals to correct problems in the video signal as it travels from one piece of equipment to another. A good "pro-camp" can reform control pulses, reset pedestal levels, correct weak color signals, and change the color phase.

Q

Quad. This is the description of the common broadcast recording system. Four heads rotate across the tape in a path perpendicular to its length. Two-inch tape is the usual standard.

R

Rack Mounting. A standard has been established for electronic component racks that are 19 inches wide. Many pieces of equipment will come with accessory brackets for such rack mounting.

Raster. The pattern described by the electron beam as it traces the 525 lines on a TV or picture tube.

Reaction Shot. A cut, either by means of a switcher or a postproduction edit, to the facial expression of a participant in a TV program.

Resolution. A measure of the amount of detail a piece of video equipment is able to display.

Rotary Erase Head. These are also called "flying erase" heads. In order for high quality editing to be done, the picture must be erased just before new picture is added to the tape. Erase heads are mounted one line away from the recording heads and pass the tape an instant before them.

S

Safe Title Area. Ninety-two percent of the TV screen, the central area.

Scoop. This is a large bowl-shaped reflector which is designed to give even illumination over a wide area as opposed to key or spot lights.

Signal-to-Noise Ratio. All equipment has a certain amount of electronic "noise" inherent in it. The ratio of this inherent noise to the signal that is being processed by the equipment is the S/N ratio. The higher this ratio, the better the quality of the sound or picture. In low-cost video, S/N ratios of 45 decibels are common. Ratios of under 40 decibels will begin to give a noticeably degraded picture.

Skew. This is the measure of the tape tension between the supply side of the machine and the capstan. Improperly adjusted tension will affect the playback picture. Consumer machines have automatically adjusted skew which needs to be periodically checked. Many 3/4" machines have manual skew controls which can be adjusted by observing the playback picture on a cross-pulse type monitor. The cross-pulse monitor is a specialized piece of equipment which displays the synchronizing pulses, normally off the edge of the picture, in the middle of the screen.

Special Effects. These refer to the processing of television signals in ways other than switching or simple fades and dissolves. Special effects encompass a whole range of elaborate manipulations of the picture, such as chroma key, moving spirals, expanding stars and circles, etc. New electronic timing control circuits are being made available all the time. Some manufacturers have libraries of plug-in modules available. Watching a network television production will bring you up to date on the latest available effects.

Special Effects Generator. This unit is often combined with an active switcher to allow fading, mixing, wipes, inserts, keys, and other ways of combining several video sources into one final program.

Subcarrier Phase Shifter. Special circuitry used to change the timing of one or more color signals so that the color hue from each source will be the same. Subcarrier phase differences are noticeable on even broadcast signals as a change in color when the studio shifts from one camera to another.

Surround Shot. This is the description of the type of camera view from within the scene itself, such as that from a portable recorder carried about in the midst of the subjects.

Switching. Moving from one video source to another. A simple "dry" switcher will connect the output of several sources, one at a time, to the input of a VTR or monitor without concern for switching in the vertical interval. This type of equipment is used in low-cost surveillance systems. A more elaborate device will make the change from one camera to another during the vertical blanking interval.

Sync. The various drive signals and pulses which keep all parts of the video system properly timed.

Sync Generator. Most pieces of video equipment have built-in sync generators which serve as internal clocks, but studios will generally use a highly accurate common source to provide pulses for the entire system. A local station, getting ready to broadcast a network program, will lock its sync generator to the sync pulses coming with the network program.

T

Tension. The pull of the capstan and pinch roller which forces the tape against the video head drum. This tension is preadjusted in consumer-type machines and is automatically maintained. A poor playback picture might indicate a need for adjustment.

Termination. Video lines should be properly terminated to keep the signal from forming standing waves in the wire. When equipment is connected properly, termination will be taken care of. Some video monitors have terminating switches which must be turned on or off to match the types of connections made. The owner's manual will describe the proper procedure. Do not leave cables which are not connected at the other end connected to your VTR while you are operating your equipment.

TBC (Time Base Corrector). Since tape can shrink, stretch, and warp, the timing pulses along one edge of the tape can change by tiny fractions of a second. This time instability is particularly noticeable in narrower tape formats. Television sets have enough timing latitude so that these slight variations do not cause noticeable problems, but this instability makes it almost impossible to link such nonbroadcast sources to the time standards demanded by broadcast television. The time base corrector does what its name implies. This is a sophisticated and complex electronic device which "saves up" the fields of the TV picture and then matches them to a new, very accurate time signal so that they will mate accurately with video information from other sources.

Time base instability is also a problem in tape copying. Timing errors will be passed on from one tape copy to the next, and each copy will add its own new problems. An agency involved in frequent tape duplication will do well to reprocess tapes through a TBC.

Trucking. Moving the camera to the right or left on its tripod and dolly.

Two-Shot. A picture that includes two people. A one-shot has only one person; three-shot, three, etc.

U

U-Format. This is the common description of the 3⁄4" cassette tapes and equipment.

UHF (Ultra High Frequency). This refers to channels 14 to 83 in the TV broadcast band—470 to 890 million cycles per second (hertz).

Umbrella. A reflecting fabric umbrella-shaped device which is used to diffuse light from a spotlight.

V

Vertical Interval Switching. The TV screen is blanked while the flying electron beam moves back to the top of the tube to begin another trace. Sophisticated editing recorders and switching equipment make the change from one program source to another during this fraction of a second.

Vidicon. This is the least expensive of the television camera picture tubes. Its advantages are low cost and reliability. Its disadvantages are limited sensitivity and lag.

Z

Zoom Lens. If you plan to work with one camera, you'll need one of these. A good zoom lens will move smoothly from a wide-angle field of view through normal view to enough telephoto or magnification to allow close-ups of persons in a scene without moving the camera. Well-designed lenses will maintain accurate focus from maximum telephoto through wide-angle. Always set focus accurately using the telephoto position; then shift the angle of view, as needed, to a wider angle. The greater depth of field at wider angles will compensate for minor tracking errors in the lens.